VOLUME 2
HOW IT WORKS

This book belongs to

_____

VOLUME 2
HOW IT WORKS

BY MARTIN L. KEEN
ILLUSTRATED BY DICK KRAMER

GROSSET & DUNLAP
A FILMWAYS COMPANY
Publishers • New York

1976 Printing
Library of Congress Catalog Card Number: 73-16657
ISBN: 0-448-12692-3 (Paperback Edition)
ISBN: 0-448-13204-4 (Library Edition)
Text copyright © 1974 by Martin L. Keen.
Illustrations copyright © 1974 by Grosset & Dunlap, Inc.
Published simultaneously in Canada.
Printed in the United States of America.

CONTENTS

INTRODUCTION

If you knew of only one machine, you would be very curious about how it works. But there are so many machines in your daily life, at home and outside, that you may easily take them for granted, never wondering about them at all. When you wind a watch, do you ever wonder what causes the clicking sound and why turning the little knob between your thumb and forefinger keeps the watch running? When you read in this book how a watch measures time accurately, second after second, year after year, you will discover that it is exciting and fascinating to understand how this small machine works. Then, the next time you wind a watch, you will find satisfaction in knowing exactly what you are doing. The same will apply when you've learned what makes an airplane fly and then see one overhead. So, too, with all the other machines described in this book.

It is not difficult to learn how a machine works. There's nothing mysterious or unknown about any of them. All machines have been thought out and constructed by human beings, and what one person can make, another person can understand.

But no matter how clearly the operation of a machine is explained, it will be better if you are able to see the working parts. A good picture may be even more helpful than seeing the machine itself, because the inside, as well as the outside, may be shown. As you read the descriptions of machines in this book, study the accompanying pictures. Doing this will make it much easier to understand how machines and other devices work.

DATA PROCESSING

You get cash register receipts at supermarkets and other stores. Some bills are mailed to your home in the form of cards with holes punched in them. Bank checks have code numbers printed at their bottoms. These three well-known things put you in contact with data processing.

In data processing, *data* are facts that are to be processed. Examples of data are the prices of things bought at a supermarket, the wages of employees of a company, the amounts on checks at a bank, the number of votes cast in each voting district during an election, the number of hairs on your head, and the number of meteors entering the earth's atmosphere in one hour. Almost any kind of records—lists, rolls, files, tables, or groups of numbers or names—can be data.

Processing is almost anything you want to do with data. If your data are numbers, you might process them by adding, subtracting, multiplying, dividing, or performing any other kind of mathematical operation with them. You can process numbers, names, or other data by arranging them in any order—for example, the test scores of a group of students, arranged in ascending order, from lowest score to highest. Or, you might arrange the names of the students in a school, either alphabetically, according to class, or according to each student's grades. Data processing also includes picking out a few pieces of data from a large amount—for instance, finding the names of employees of a company who lost working time because of illness in February. Processing includes any other kind of operations upon data, such as making out a payroll, finding the balance in the account of a customer of a bank, or using data broadcast from a manned spacecraft to determine how astronauts should guide their craft.

Processed data provide *information*. Suppose you want to find the sum of 1 plus 1. The two 1's are the data. You process the data by adding the 1's, and get the sum, 2. The 2 is the information. The 2 might now become part of data if you want to find the sum of 2 plus 1. In making out a payroll, data would include the name of each employee, the department in which he works, the number of hours he worked during the pay period, his social security number, deductions for his social security payments, the number of dependents he may have, his withholding tax deductions, deductions for bonds bought on a payroll savings plan, and deductions for his medical insurance. The data will be processed by adding, subtracting, and putting items in proper order. The information will be the amount of pay due an employee and will be printed on his paycheck. Then the checks will be grouped according to department and, in each department, arranged in alphabetical order.

Data put into a processing machine is called *input*. Processed data in the form of information is *output*.

When finding the sum of, say, 5 plus 3, you can process the data mentally by thinking of what the sum of 5 added to 3 is; or you can count it out on your fingers; or you can use a pencil to add the numbers on a piece of paper. But when we refer to data processing in general, we mean *automatic data processing*. People put data into machines, and then the machines do the processing without further help from them. The main advantages of data processing are (1) speed, (2) storage of large amounts of data that are always ready for quick processing, and (3) accuracy: machines make fewer errors than do people.

Speed is probably the most important advantage of automatic data processing. In the census of 1880, when the United States had a population of 50,000,000 people, it took 7½ years to process the facts gathered by census takers. In the 1890 census, the United States Census Bureau used punched-card automatic data processing. Although the population had increased to 63,000,000 and the data processing machines were crude, the census data was processed in 2½ years. In 1970, electronic data processing machines were used to process census data gathered from a population of 207,000,000. This task took less than a year and many more kinds of information were obtained from the data.

The machines that process data are called *hardware*. The materials upon which the machines work and the printed rules according to which they work are *software*. Software includes punch cards, paper and plastic tapes, the large sheets of paper called coding sheets, printout sheets on which processed data are printed, computer routines and programs, and technical manuals for operating the machines.

PUNCHED CARDS

The piece of software that is probably the most widely used in data processing is the *punched card* (Fig. 1), a rectangular piece of cardboard. The card most generally used is 7⅜ inches long, 3¼ inches wide, and 7/1000 inch thick. Printed on one side of the card are 12 *rows* of numbers arranged in 80 *columns*. Each column has 0 (zero) at the top and 9 at the bottom. The columns are numbered from left to right in two rows of small numbers, one below the 0's row and one below the 9's row. These small numbers are there to make it easy to find a particular column without having to count from the left-hand column. Some cards make it even easier by having five rows of small numbers.

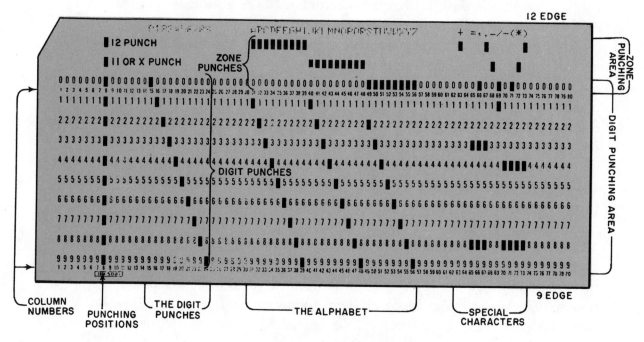

FIGURE 1

Data is transferred to a card by punching holes in it with a *keypunch machine*. Each punch cuts a small rectangular hole in the card. Except for punches made above the 0's row, where there are no numbers, each punch cuts a number out of the card. (The rows of small guide numbers are never punched.) The numbers in the columns are called *positions*. For example, if the 8 is punched, the punch is said to be in the "8 position."

The data punched into a card is *alphanumeric*, which means that the data may consist of either letters (*alpha*betic) or numbers (*numeric*). Usually, both letters and numbers are needed. For example, the

14

letters may make up the name of an employee and the numbers his weekly salary. "Alphanumeric" usually is abbreviated as "alphameric."

Since there are no letters on a card, a system of using numbers to represent letters had to be devised. Alphabetic punching requires two extra rows, the *12's row* and the *11's row* (sometimes called the X *row*). These two rows are not usually printed on the card because the upper area is reserved for printed headings, as when the card is used as a bill. Or, the upper area may be used for printing the data that is punched in the card. For alphabetic punching, a third row (in addition to the 12's and 11's rows) is needed, and the 0's row is used. These three rows are called *zones*. By combining a zone punch with a column punch, the letters of the alphabet can be punched into a card. The combinations are:

ZONE/ POSITION	LETTER	ZONE/ POSITION	LETTER	ZONE/ POSITION	LETTER
					(no punch in the 1's position)
12-1	A	11-1	J		
12-2	B	11-2	K	0-2	S
12-3	C	11-3	L	0-3	T
12-4	D	11-4	M	0-4	U
12-5	E	11-5	N	0-5	V
12-6	F	11-6	O	0-6	W
12-7	G	11-7	P	0-7	X
12-8	H	11-8	Q	0-8	Y
12-9	I	11-9	R	0-9	Z

In Figure 1, columns 31 to 56 represent the letters A to Z.

Numbers are punched without any zone punch. The punches in columns 15 to 24 represent the numbers 0 to 9.

Special characters, such as &, =, ?, and others, consist of one, two, or three punches in a column. The punch positions ensure that they cannot be confused with alphanumeric punches. For example, a 12 punch alone is "&." A 6 punch and 8 punch in the same column stand for "=." And 0, 7, and 8 all punched in the same column mean "?." To punch any character requiring more than one numeric punch in the same column, the keypunch machine operator holds down a key marked MULT PCH (multiple punch). If it isn't necessary to punch anything in a column, a key is pressed that skips that column.

Suppose you want to punch into a card the data, "523 KEYPUNCH MACHINES?" The card would look like the one in Figure 2.

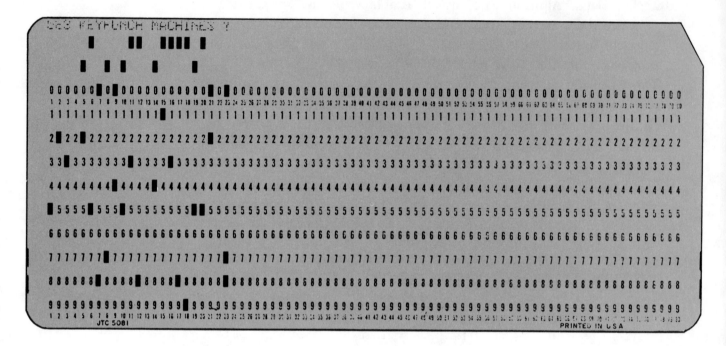

FIGURE 2

Some keypunch machines print at the top of the card whatever is punched in the card (Fig. 1).

KEYPUNCH MACHINE

Figure 3 shows a keypunch machine and its keyboard. These machines are also called cardpunch machines. The keypunch operator sits at the machine and strikes the keys in the same way a typist strikes the keys of a typewriter. The operator takes data from records such as bills, invoices, airplane-seat charts, class rosters, or payrolls. By striking the proper keys, the operator transfers data from the written records to the punch cards.

The keypunch machine is connected to a source of electric current, and the punching is done by electric power. A hole is punched in a card by a *punching knife*, which is part of a punching unit. (Fig. 4 shows this unit in simplified form.) When the operator presses a key, electric current flows through the coils of an *electromagnet*, causing it to attract and pull down the *armature*. This action pushes down the *punching bail*,

16

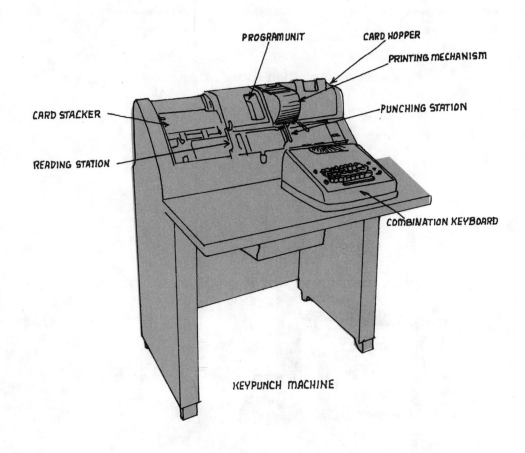

KEYPUNCH MACHINE

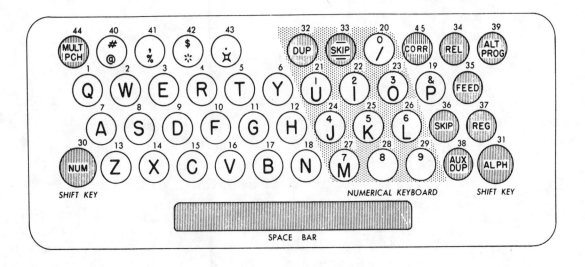

FIGURE 3

which, in turn, pushes down the *punch*. The knife on the end of the punch cuts a hole in the card. The *stop* keeps the punch from moving down too far. The punching action cuts off the electric current and the electromagnet no longer pulls on the armature. The *return spring* attached to the bail pulls it up, and the *punch-restoring* bail pushes the punch upward, readying it for another punch.

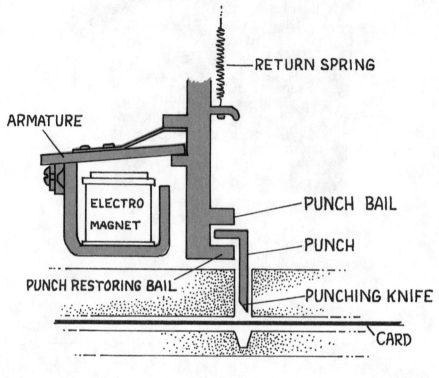

FIGURE 4

When a card is completely punched, the operator strikes the key marked FEED, which causes the machine to move a card (from a storage hopper) to a position behind the card to be punched. The card that was in this position is moved to the punching position, or *punching station*. The card just punched is moved to the *reading station*. And the card in front of the one at the reading station is stacked in a collecting bin.

VERIFIER

Processing data with punched cards may include hundreds or thousands of cards. Correcting an error after the cards have been processed can be costly because it will lose much of the time gained by machine processing. It's important, therefore, to catch an error as early in the processing as possible. To catch errors in punched cards, a machine called a *verifier* is used. It looks like a keypunch machine and has the same alphanumeric keyboard. Within the verifier there are no punching knives. Instead, there are blunt pins.

Punched cards are put into the hopper of the verifier in the same order in which they were punched. The machine moves them, one at a time, into the *verifying station*, which is in the same place as the punching station of a keypunch machine. The verifier operator reads the same data records the keypunch operator read, and then strikes the keys as if he were punching a card.

Pressing a key on the verifier causes a pin within the machine to move at the card in the same way the punching knife did. The card rests against a metal plate (Fig. 5). If a punched hole is in front of the pin, it passes through the card and touches the plate, completing an electrical circuit. The pin is withdrawn from the hole and the card is moved one column to the left. If the pin should strike a column position that was not punched, the card acts as an electrical insulator and no circuit is completed. When this happens, the machine stops and locks in position, and a light above the keyboard flashes on.

It is not too likely that both the keypunch operator and the verifier operator would make the same mistake at the same position on a card, but in case it should happen, the machine operator has two more chances to get agreement between the verifying keystroke and the original keypunch. If there is no agreement, the top edge of the column being verified is notched by the machine. This identifies the column in which the error was made. If a card passes through the verifier without showing an error, the card is notched at the right edge opposite the 1's row.

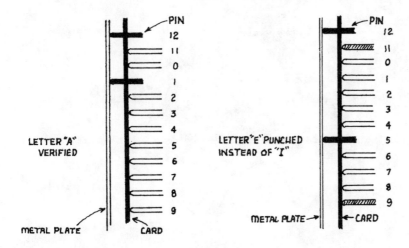

FIGURE 5

To correct an error, a completely new card may be punched. Or, a small patch may be pasted over each error and the proper position then punched by means of a hand-punch or by putting the card back into a keypunch machine.

READING PUNCHED CARDS

The purpose of punching a card and verifying it is to use the card as part of an *automatic* data process. If punched cards had to be read by human operators, the cards wouldn't be any more useful than pieces of paper with data typed on them, but punched cards can be read by machines—which then act according to the data they read. When dealing with punched cards, the word "read" means to translate punches into impulses of electric current that control the working of machines. For example, a punched card sorter reads cards and sorts them in any order desired. Several hundred payroll cards may be sorted according to the first letter of each employee's last name.

One way of reading punched cards is to pass each card over a metal roller, or drum. Eighty small metal brushes press upon the card, one brush on each column (Fig. 6). The roller is connected to a source of electric current. No current can pass through the card. But when the card has moved to a position in which a punch-hole is beneath a brush, current flows from the drum to the brush. From the brush the current goes to some other location in the machine where it causes a lever, wheel, cam, switch, or some other mechanical unit to move as part of the working of the machine.

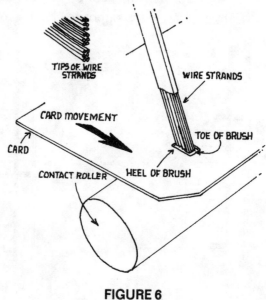

FIGURE 6

A second way in which punched cards are automatically read makes use of a photocell. (To learn how a photocell works, see the section on PHOTOELECTRIC CELL, or ELECTRIC EYE in this book.) A transport roller moves a punched card in front of a beam of light (Fig. 7). Behind the card is a column of 12 photocells, one for each row. Wherever a punch hole appears in a card, light can pass through to the photocell, generating an electric current which is transmitted to a particular part of the machine.

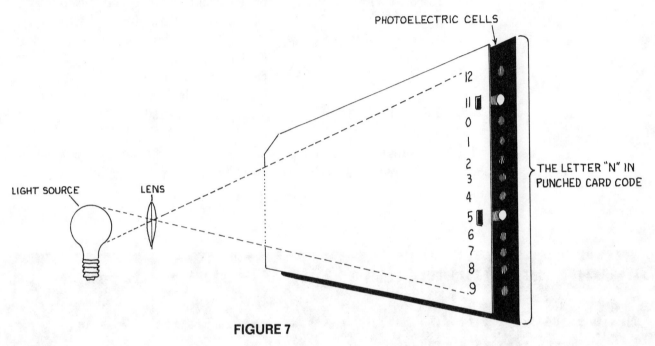

FIGURE 7

PUNCHED-CARD CONTROL

Once we understand that punched cards can be read by data processing machines, it is easy to see that the cards can be used to control any machines powered by electricity. Since the holes in the cards start or stop the flow of current through electric circuits, the data punched in the cards can control the machines. One example of punched-card control is the *program card*, a card with coded punches that controls a keypunch machine automatically.

Punched cards are usually divided into groups of columns, which are called *fields*. For example, the first three columns of a card might be used to indicate the department number of an employee. These columns make up the field. The next field on the same card might show the employee's social security number.

21

In a program card, the 12 punch is called the *field definer*. It is punched in all columns of a field, except the first, to signal how many columns the field includes. The punch in the first column is the *action code*. It signals the machine to skip, duplicate, or leave blank all columns in which the field definer is punched. The most common control instructions punched into a program card are:

COLUMN POSITION PUNCHED	SIGNALS MACHINE TO:
12 (field definer)	punch what the action code calls for
11	start automatic skipping
0	start automatic duplication
1	shift to alphabetic punching
5	end of [data be punched on] card
No punch (press SPACE Key)	leave field blank and allow operator to punch new data

Figure 8 shows a punched program card. By referring to the table above, you can see how the program card will signal the keypunch machine to punch new cards.

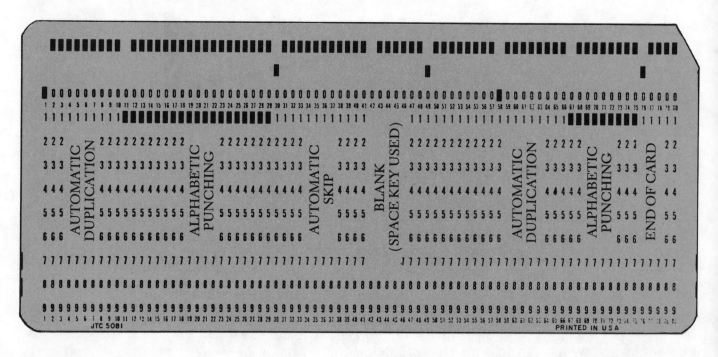

FIGURE 8

22

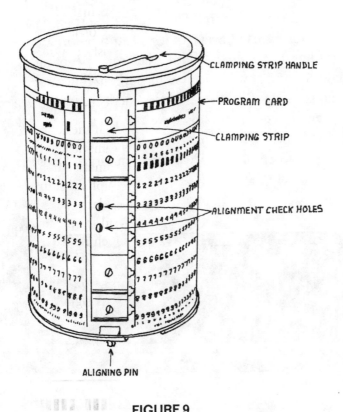

CLAMPING STRIP HANDLE

PROGRAM CARD

CLAMPING STRIP

ALIGNMENT CHECK HOLES

ALIGNING PIN

FIGURE 9

To use a program card to control a keypunch machine, the card is wound around a drum (Fig. 9) and clamped in place. The drum is inserted into the machine. The drum revolves in step with the movement of each card past the reading and punching stations of the keypunch machine. The reading brushes read the punches in the program card and signal the punching knives where to punch data in the columns. They also signal transport rollers how far to move the card.

Punched cards can be used not only to control the punching of other cards but also to control manufacturing procedures and any other operation that depends on electricity, such as the dialing of telephone numbers. An example of punched card control in manufacturing is the control of automatic drilling machines. A drilling machine in an automobile factory may have 20 drills in 4 rows of 5 columns. When a certain automobile part is moved to a position beneath the drills, a program card may signal drills in row 2, column 1, row 3, column 5, and row 5, columns 1 and 4, to drill holes in the part.

SORTER

A third advantage of punched card data over typewritten data is in the very rapid sorting of data. The speed of sorting a large number of typewritten cards by hand averages less than 6 per minute. An automatic punched card sorter can do the job at 2,000 cards per minute.

Suppose a company has a file of several thousand punched cards that contain the names, addresses, department numbers, wages, and other data on its employees. The cards have not been sorted in any way; they are in random order. The company has 99 departments and the cards are to be arranged according to department number. Department numbers are punched in columns 1 and 2. Let's see how a sampling of ten cards would be sorted.

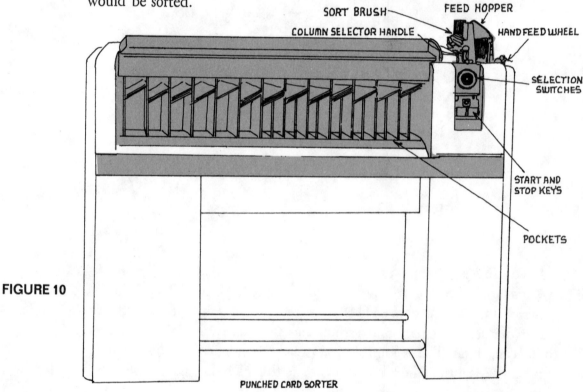

FIGURE 10

PUNCHED CARD SORTER

The card sorter (Fig. 10) has 13 bins, or *pockets*, into which the cards are separated. The pockets correspond to the 10 column numbers, plus zones 11 and 12. The thirteenth pocket is the "R," or reject, bin. Into it go cards not properly punched for the data being sorted. The sorter also has selection switches, which enable us to set the machine for sorting either by numerical or zone punches. We can also set the reading brushes to read any specific column. We put the punched cards into the feed hopper and set the switches for numerical sorting. Our ten cards are in the order shown in Figure 11-A. (We read from bottom to top.) We

24

A. NUMBERS ON TEN CARDS   98
    BEFORE SORTING   20
                        12
                        51
                        85
                        37
                        45   FIGURE 11-A
                        23
                        31
                        42

set the brushes to read column 2, because we want to sort the cards according to the units, or right-hand, digit of each number. We push the starter key. The sorter reads the punches in column 2 of each card and drops it into a pocket according to the units digit read. At the end of this first sorting, the cards are located in the pockets as shown in Figure 11-B.

B. LOCATION OF CARDS IN POCKETS
   AFTER FIRST SORTING

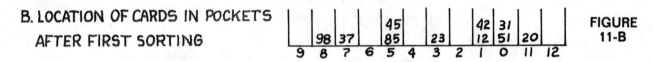

FIGURE 11-B

The cards are taken out of the pockets, starting with the right-hand pocket. They are in the order in which they were taken from the pockets, with those from the right-hand pocket on the bottom. Figure 11-C shows the order of the cards when stacked after the first sorting pass.

C. ORDER OF CARDS AS STACKED
   AFTER FIRST SORTING   98
                        37
                        45
                        85
                        23
                        42
                        12   FIGURE 11-C
                        31
                        51
                        20

The cards are put into the feed hopper again and the brushes are set to read column 1, which indicates the 10's digits of our set of numbers. The results of the second pass through the sorter are shown in Figures 11-D and E. The cards are now in numerical order. For sorting numbers having more than two digits, the cards would be sorted as many times as there are digits.

Since alphabetical data can be punched into cards, a sorter can sort alphabetically. In alphabetical sorting, we start with the first letter of the words or names punched in the field we are sorting. This means that the reading brushes are set to read the leftmost column first, and then the next column to the right. Since a letter requires both a numerical and a zone punch, we must pass the cards through the sorter twice for each letter.

FIGURE 11-D

D. LOCATIONS OF CARDS IN POCKETS AFTER SECOND SORTING.

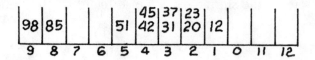

FIGURE 11-E

E. CARDS STACKED IN PROPER NUMERICAL ORDER AFTER SECOND SORTING.

98
85
51
45
42
37
31
23
20
12

INSIDE THE SORTER

Punched cards are pulled from the feed hopper by rubber-rimmed rollers. Immediately upon leaving the stack, a card passes over a contact roller (Fig. 12) for reading. If the reading brush falls through a hole and makes contact with the roller, an electric circuit is completed. Two coils of an electromagnet pull down a metal plate that is called an *armature*. This allows all chute blades not held up by the card to drop. The card then passes over the first one of those chute blades that dropped. The number and order of this chute blade corresponds to the digit punched in

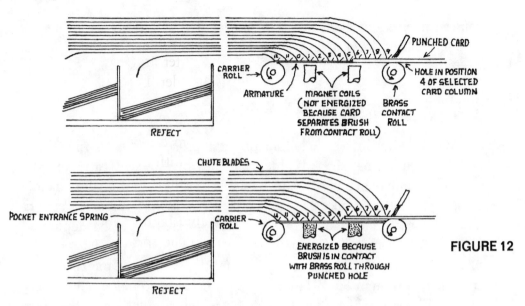

FIGURE 12

the card. Carrier rollers move the card along the chute until it reaches the end of the blade and falls into a pocket. The blade ends at a pocket that has the same number as the blade. If an unpunched card or one punched in the wrong column is fed into the sorter, the card acts as an insulator, preventing the brush from making contact with the roller. The armature does not act, and the card passes all the chutes and falls into the reject pocket.

In the upper part of Figure 12, a card with a punch in the 4 position has not yet reached the reading brushes and the leading edge is passing under the chute blades. In the lower part of the illustration, the 4 punch has reached the reading brush and an electrical contact has been made. The electromagnets have pulled down the armature and all the chutes in front of number 5 have dropped. The card is just beginning to move into the open chute, which is number 4. It will move along the chute until it falls into pocket number 4.

Another way of opening a chute for passage of a card is shown in Figure 13. When the hole passes the reading brush, the electric circuit

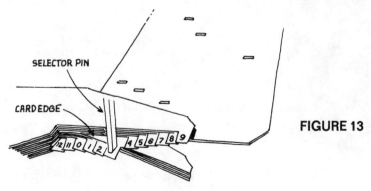

FIGURE 13

causes an electromagnet to move one of 12 *selector pins* downward. The pin pushes down upon a chute-blade tab, opening the chute for the card.

AUTOMATIC REPRODUCING PUNCH

Another way in which automatic data processing saves time is by automatic punching of cards. Identical files of punched cards may be needed in more than one place, for example, several departments of a large company, different offices of a government bureau, or army posts at various locations throughout a country. Files of cards could be duplicated by keypunch machines using program cards, but it would be far too slow. A card at a time would go through the machine as it was punched from column 1 to column 80. A faster way is to use an *automatic reproducing punch* (Fig. 14), which uses 80 knives to punch at one time all the numbers needed in any row, as the card moves through the machine from top to bottom. This machine will also *gangpunch* files of cards, which means that it will punch data from a master card into as many more cards as are needed.

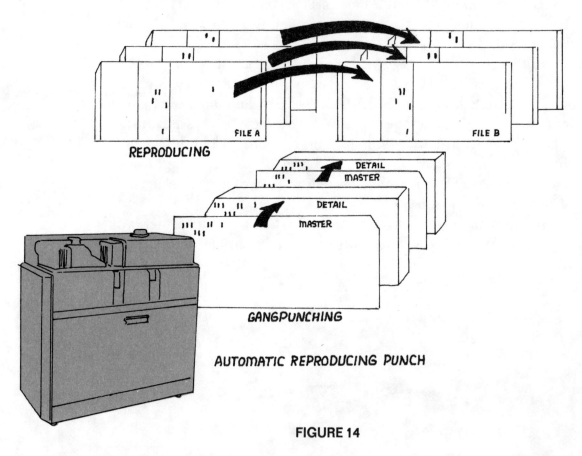

FIGURE 14

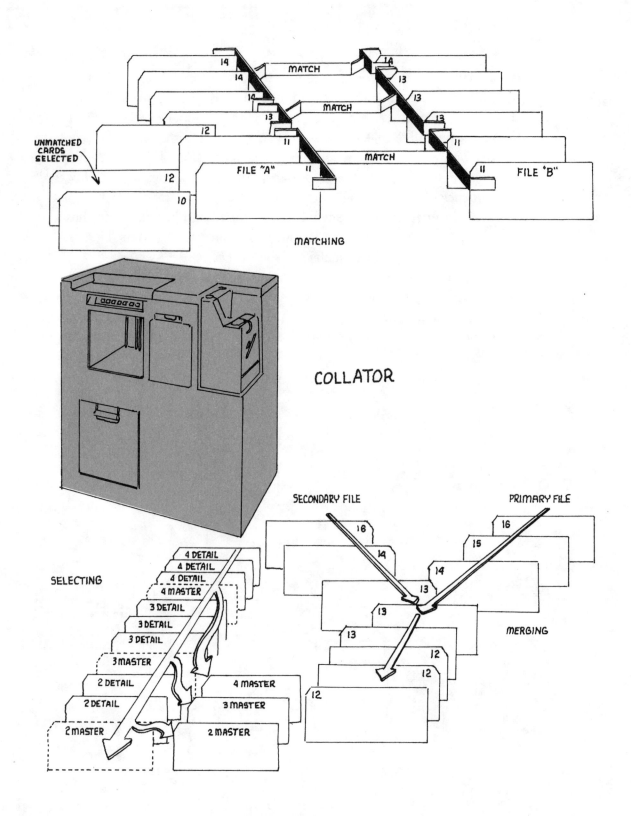

FIGURE 15

COLLATOR

Suppose you want to combine into one file two files of punched cards that are in numerical or alphabetical sequence. You could place both files together and sort them in a sorter. This would work, but it is slow. Also, suppose you have two files of cards in sequence and you want to make a single file that contains only some of the cards. You could not do this with a sorter; you would need a *collator* (Fig. 15). Combining two files of cards is called *merging*. Besides merging, a collator can *check the sequence* of data punched into a file of cards, to see if the cards are in order. It can *match* cards in one file with those of another, rejecting those that do not match. It can select from a file cards with certain kinds of data, and not change the sequence of the others.

Figure 16-A shows the working scheme of a collator. What is important is that there are three reading stations. Two sets of reading brushes (marked *sequence read* and *primary read*) make it possible to compare cards moving out of the *primary feed hopper*. To compare means to

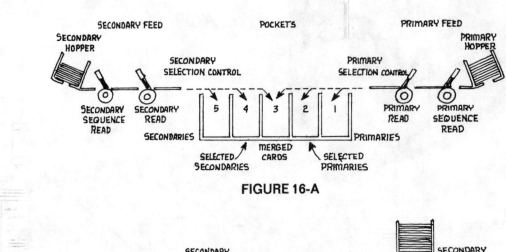

FIGURE 16-A

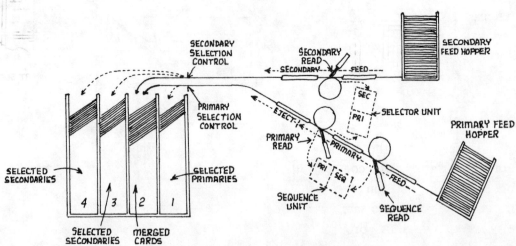

FIGURE 16-B

read whether one number is lower, equal to, or higher than another number. This explains why cards moving out of the primary feed hopper pass over two sets of brushes. The set of brushes marked *secondary read* reads cards from the *secondary feed hopper*. This enables the collator to compare cards in two separate files, then match or merge them, or select one or more cards from a file (Fig. 16-B).

AUTOMATIC DATA PROCESSING SYSTEMS

The use of the machines we have been describing is usually aimed at one target: printing on paper information that results from processing data. The information may be a bill, a payroll, a schedule of freight-car loadings, a scientific report, or a school's daily attendance record. The machines are used in a definite order, or *system* (Figure 17).

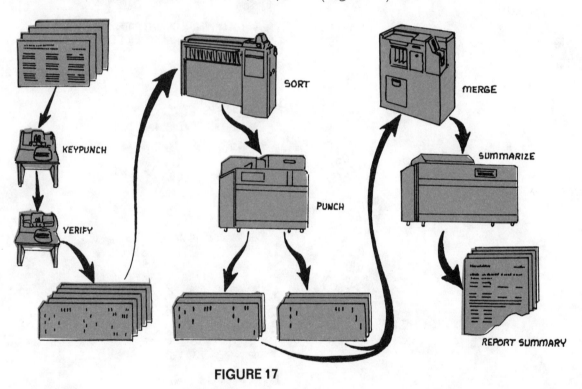

FIGURE 17

At the end of the system is an *end-of-line* machine. It may be a billing machine, an accounting machine, or some other machine that prints the information obtained from processing data. All end-of-line machines work on the same electrical principles as other automatic data processing machines. Brushes read punched cards, and the electrical impulses that flow from the card reader move print chains, print wheels (Fig. 18), electric-typewriter keys, or other printing devices.

31

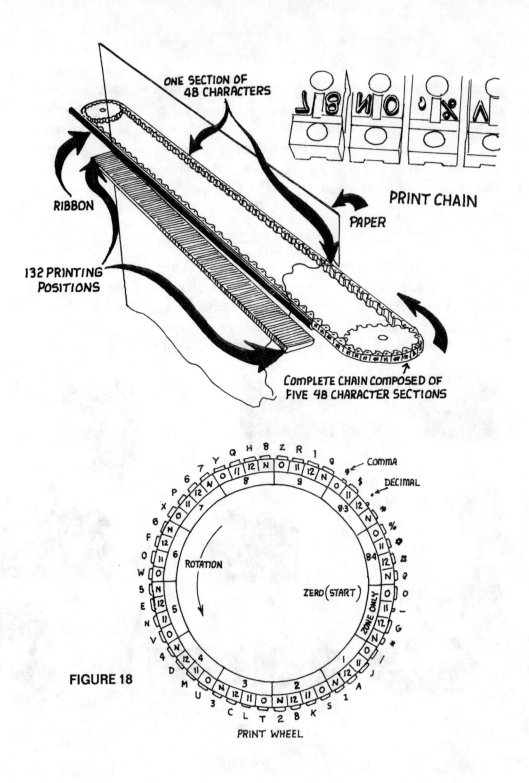

ONE SECTION OF 48 CHARACTERS

PRINT CHAIN

RIBBON

PAPER

132 PRINTING POSITIONS

COMPLETE CHAIN COMPOSED OF FIVE 48 CHARACTER SECTIONS

COMMA

DECIMAL

ROTATION

ZERO (START)

ZONE ONLY

FIGURE 18

PRINT WHEEL

CONTROL PANELS, OR PLUGBOARDS

We have seen that automatic card punches, sorters, and collators can perform more than one kind of operation. To change from one kind to another, a machine must have its electric circuits changed. This means that some parts of the machine must be rewired. To take the machine apart and change the wiring would be a ridiculously slow and costly task. Instead, rewiring is done by means of *control panels*, or *plugboards*. Data processing machines are constructed so that a point in every circuit is wired to an immovable panel, called the *machine panel*, on the side of the machine. On the inner side of the panel, each circuit ends in a connection to a small cylinder that passes through the panel, two arrangements of which are shown in Figs. 19 and 20. The outside of each cylinder

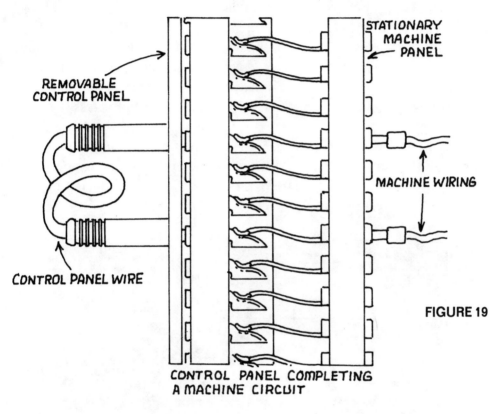

REMOVABLE
CONTROL PANEL

STATIONARY
MACHINE
PANEL

MACHINE WIRING

CONTROL PANEL WIRE

FIGURE 19

CONTROL PANEL COMPLETING
A MACHINE CIRCUIT

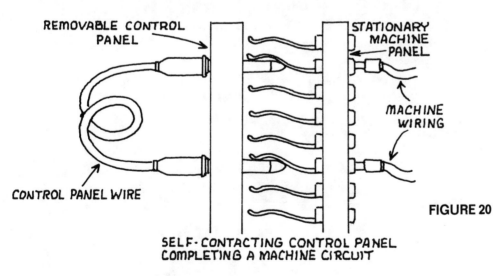

REMOVABLE CONTROL
PANEL

STATIONARY
MACHINE
PANEL

MACHINE
WIRING

CONTROL PANEL WIRE

FIGURE 20

SELF-CONTACTING CONTROL PANEL
COMPLETING A MACHINE CIRCUIT

extends as a springy metal prong, called a *jack*. There are several hundred of these in a panel. Another panel, called a *removable panel*, or *plugboard*, fits over the machine panel. There are as many metal-rimmed holes—called *hubs*—in the plugboard as there are jacks in the machine panel. On the inner side of the plugboard, the holes form tapered half-cylinders. The inner end of each half-cylinder in the plugboard slips under one of the prongs of a jack in the machine panel. The springy prongs hold the plugboard firmly. Plugs attached to each end of removable wires fit into the hubs. When the plugs are pushed into hubs, the wires become parts of the machine's electrical circuits. The wires are in half a dozen different lengths, and each length has its own color. The person who wires the plugboard usually carries the wires around in a sort of tool box. To find a wire of the length needed, he simply picks out one of the proper color.

To wire a machine for a particular operation, the plugboard wirer first pulls the plugboard off the side of the machine. Then he removes the wires plugged into the hubs. His job of rewiring is one of completing circuits with wire connections which he plugs into hubs.

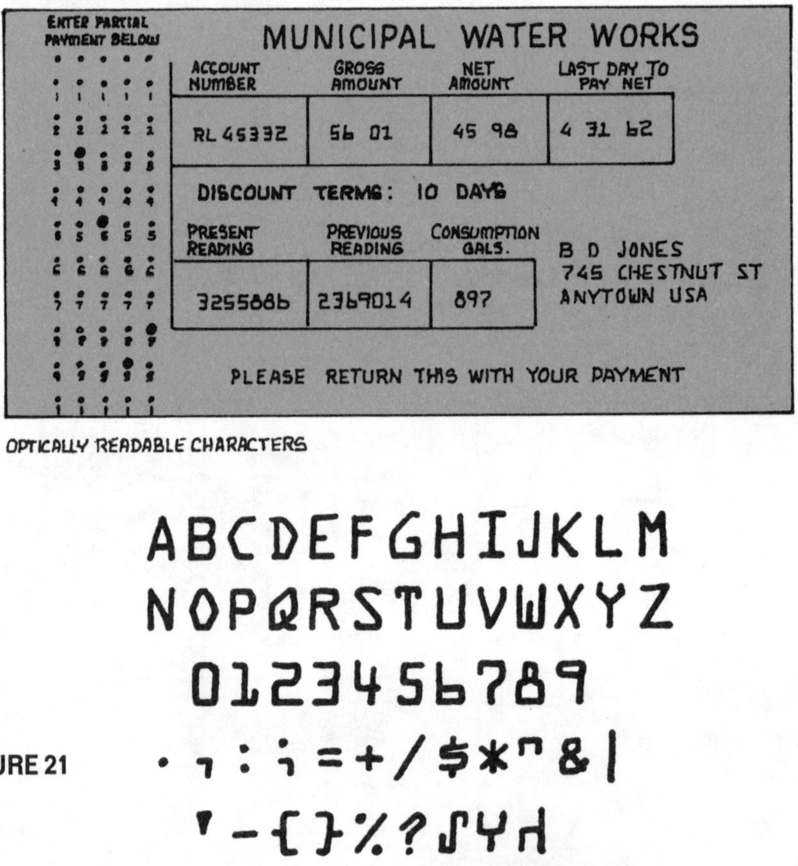

OPTICALLY READABLE CHARACTERS

FIGURE 21

OPTICAL CHARACTER READERS

Bills, checks, multiple-choice examination answers, and other kinds of printed matter can be read by certain machines. One of these is the *optical character reader.*

Figure 21 shows a bill, and below the bill are an alphabet of upper-case (capital) letters and the numbers 0 to 9 typed in specially formed characters. At the left-hand side of the bill are five columns of numbers. Above each number (except zero) is a circle that can be filled in by pencil.

There are a number of different kinds of optical character readers. In one kind, one bill at a time is moved from a feed hopper through a brightly lighted chamber of the machine. Light reflected from the bill is guided by lenses to a vertical row of twelve photocells (Fig. 22) . There

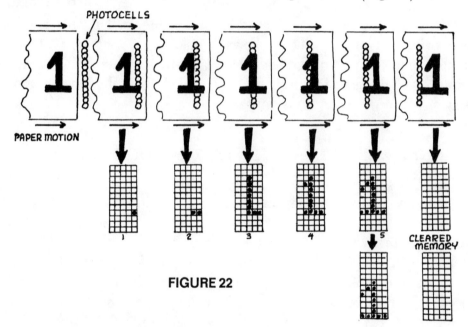

FIGURE 22

also is a rectangle made up of five vertical rows with twelve squares in each row. The rectangle is a *character matrix.* Each square is composed of a material that can store an electric charge. There is one matrix for each row of print to be read by the machine. The ink in which each character is printed reflects very little light; the rest of the surface of the paper reflects much light to the photocells. No electric current is produced by the photocells that receive little light. Strong current is produced by the cells that receive much reflected light.

In the upper row of Figure 22, the number "1" is shown as it passes the column of photocells. The middle row shows the number of positive (+) electric charges increasing in a matrix until a whole character appears. The electric charge patterns of the letters A to Z and the numbers 0 to 9 are stored in a unit of the machine. A control unit compares the character being built up in the matrix with the characters in the machine's storage, or memory. By the time the last part of a character has passed the column of photocells, the optical character reader has matched the pattern in the matrix with one in the memory. The moment a stored pattern matches one coming from the character matrix, the machine sends this single piece of data to another part of the machine. More than 2,000 characters per second can be read in this manner. The use made of the data read by the optical character reader depends upon the specific type of data processing machine the reader is part of.

If a bill has been only partly paid and this fact is to become part of processed data, a clerk fills in circles on the left side of the bill, indicating the amount paid. This is done before the bill is put into the optical character reader. In Figure 21, the bill is for $45.98, but only $35.98 was paid. The amount paid is shown by the filled-in circles. Light reflected from this part of the bill goes to a matrix of photocells, and the positions of the filled-in circles are compared and matched in the same way as when the reader reads printing.

MAGNETIC INK CHARACTER RECOGNITION SYSTEM (MICR)

The ink used for printing the numbers and symbols on the bottoms of checks contains very fine particles of iron oxide, a substance that is very easily magnetized. The bottom of the check is divided into three fields (Fig. 23). At the left is the *check routing and transit number field*. It shows your bank's number and a routing number. These numbers are needed to make certain that all checks belonging to your bank are returned to it after they have been sent from bank to bank and then processed at a central bank called a *clearinghouse*. The middle group of numbers is the *on us field*, which shows your account number at your bank. The numbers in these fields are printed on blank checks by the company that manufactures the checks. The field at the right is the *amount field*, which indicates the amount of the check. This field is blank until a check comes into a bank for payment.

When a check comes into a bank, it eventually goes to the bookkeeping department, where batches of checks are put into the feed hopper of a machine that has a keyboard with special magnetic-ink characters—numbers and symbols—as shown at left. An operator seated at the machine presses a key that causes a check to be moved from the

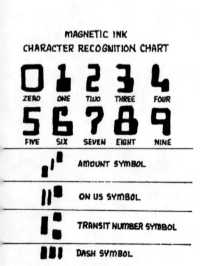

MAGNETIC INK
CHARACTER RECOGNITION CHART

0 1 2 3 4
ZERO ONE TWO THREE FOUR

5 6 7 8 9
FIVE SIX SEVEN EIGHT NINE

AMOUNT SYMBOL

ON US SYMBOL

TRANSIT NUMBER SYMBOL

DASH SYMBOL

36

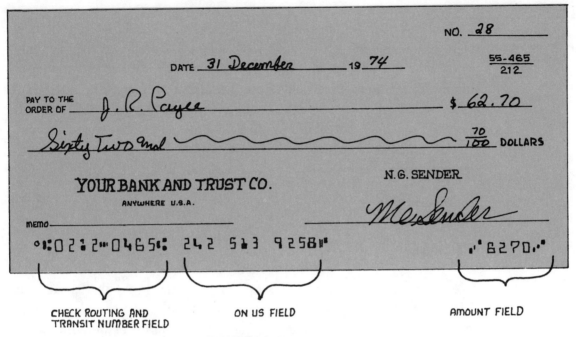

CHECK ROUTING AND
TRANSIT NUMBER FIELD   ON US FIELD   AMOUNT FIELD

FIGURE 23

hopper to a reading station above the keyboard. The operator reads the check, strikes the proper keys, and the machine prints the amount of the check in the amount field. The printing is done in magnetic ink. When all the checks have passed through the machine, they are sent to the clearinghouse.

At the clearinghouse, checks are put into a *reader-sorter*. When the checks are at the reading station of this machine, they are in a strong magnetic field—a space containing lines of magnetic force. The special ink becomes magnetized. Behind the bottom line of a check are devices, called *sensors*, that can sense the shape of lines of magnetic force. Each number and symbol printed in magnetic ink produces a differently shaped set of magnetic force lines. The sensors translate the different shapes into electrical impulses of varying patterns. The impulses go to the control unit of the reader-sorter, where they are matched with patterns stored in the machine. A matching is completed in less than 1/100,000 of a second. When impulse patterns match, the control unit causes a printing key to print the matched number in ordinary ink and numbers on a sheet of paper.

In the clearinghouse, MICR reader-sorters print lists of checks, and calculate and print each bank's clearinghouse balance. The machines also sort the checks according to the characters printed in the check routing and transit number field. This printed information, along with the sorted checks, are returned to the bank on which the checks were drawn.

Bank tellers sometimes make pencil marks on checks as they handle them. Smudges and other marks may also accidentally appear. If such marks were to fall near the bottom of the check, and if the numbers comprising the processing fields were printed in ordinary ink, an optical reader might misread the data contained in the numbers or it might reject the marked-up or smudged check as unreadable. But with numbers printed in magnetic ink, the MICR reader-sorter will read only the numbers and ignore the other marks and smudges.

COMPUTERS

Most people know computers as electronic machines that make out charge-account bills and solve complicated arithmetic problems in a second or two. This is a somewhat general description of only one kind of computer, but it does disclose an important fact about electronic computers: they are fast. Not all computers are electronic, however, and they do much more than make out bills and solve arithmetic problems.

Punched-card data processing machines and calculating machines, such as adding machines, are electromechanical machines. They contain many mechanical parts, such as keys, punching knives, carrier rolls, chute blades, armatures, and printing devices. These are moved by the power of electric current. Although these parts move very fast, it takes time to start, move, and stop them. Electronic computers, too, are powered by electric current, but they have no moving parts. For this reason, they can work almost as fast as the speed at which electric current can flow through them—186,000 miles (or almost 12,000,000,000 inches) per second. This explains why electronic devices work so fast.

The extreme speed of electronic computers makes it possible for them to perform a large number of mathematical operations in a short time. For example, suppose you want to calculate $1,780,256 \times 864,793$. If you were to do this multiplication using pencil and paper, it would take you between four and five minutes. Using an electromechanical calculating machine, the result would be obtained in about six seconds. An electronic computer would do the same calculation in less than 1/1000 of a second. The computer would add 1,780,256 to itself 864,793 times (because multiplication is the equivalent of making a series of additions). The computer can operate this quickly because it can perform a single addition in one-billionth of a second.

All computers may be divided into two kinds: *analog* and *digital*.

ANALOG COMPUTERS

If one thing looks or acts like another, the first *simulates* the second. For example, a pump simulates a heart, an airplane simulates a bird, and a camera simulates an eye. If one thing simulates another, the two things are *analogs* of each other. A pump is an analog of a heart, and so on.

Because a map simulates an area on the earth's surface, it is an analog of that area. Suppose you have a map upon which a length of one inch equals five miles of distance in the area covered by the map, and you want to know the straight-line distance between Browntown and Greenville. Place the end of a ruler on the dot that locates Browntown, and note the number of inches between that and the Greenville dot. By multiplying this number by five, the product will be the number of miles from Browntown to Greenville.

You could speed up the map-reading process by constructing a special ruler which would be a simple analog computer. The ruler would have the one-inch divisions labeled by 5's, and each one-inch division would be divided into five parts (Fig. 24). Then each small division on the ruler would be the analog of one mile on the map. To compute, you would only have to place the ruler properly on the map to know instantly the distance between any two points. The new ruler is an analog computer because it *automatically* provides the answer to reading distances on the map. In this simple analog computer, the input is the physical quantity distance, or length. The output is the number of miles between places on the surface of the earth.

A slide rule is another simple analog computer. It multiplies and divides by adding and subtracting lengths between marks on a pair of scales, one of which slides along the other (Fig. 24). The lengths are proportional to the values of the logarithms of the numbers printed on the scales. Thus, the lengths are physical quantities that are analogs of numbers. When you slide the scales according to certain rules, you perform analogs of multiplying or dividing by means of logarithms. The advantage of a slide rule is the same as that of most computers: speed. Once you have placed the slide in proper position, the answer to the calculation (output) may be seen instantaneously. This, of course, is much simpler and faster than making the same calculation by using tables of logarithms.

Although the map-and-ruler and slide rule are true analog computers, they differ from most analog computers because the quantities that they use remain unchanged before and during the time you are using these

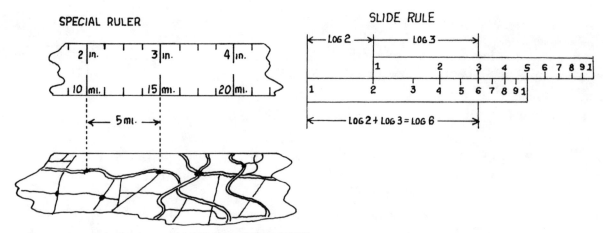

SPECIAL RULER

2 in.   3 in.   4 in.

10 mi.   15 mi.   20 mi.

← 5 mi. →

LENGTHS ON SPECIAL RULER ARE ANALOGS OF DISTANCES ON MAP

SLIDE RULE

← LOG 2 →   ← LOG 3 →

1   2   3   4   5   6 7 8 9 1

1   2   3   4   5   6 7 8 9 1

← LOG 2 + LOG 3 = LOG 6 →

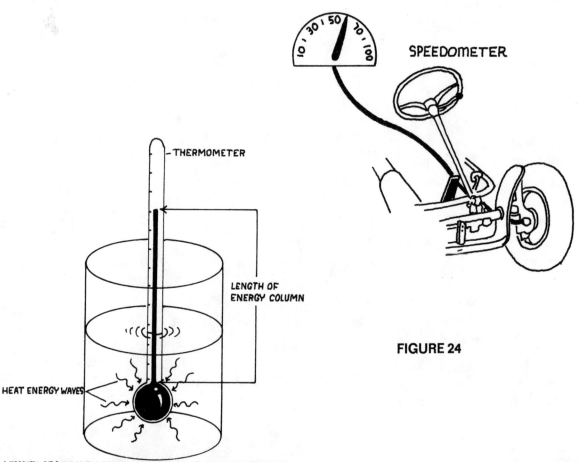

SPEEDOMETER

10 30 50 70 100

— THERMOMETER

LENGTH OF
ENERGY COLUMN

HEAT ENERGY WAVES

FIGURE 24

LENGTH OF MERCURY COLUMN IS ANALOG OF SUM OF ENERGY OF
MOLECULES OF THE LIQUID, WHICH IS THE HOTNESS OR TEMPERATURE
OF THE LIQUID.

40

computers. The inputs of most analog computers consist of *continuously changing* physical quantities, such as length (or distance), force of an electric current (voltage), intensity of sound or light, the number of turns of a wheel or shaft in a unit of time, and others. By "continuously changing," we mean that the physical quantity changes smoothly, without any breaks or gaps. For example, if the physical quantity is distance, and an object, say an airplane, moves 100 miles, it passes through every possible fraction of the 100 miles, from 0 to 100. Or, suppose the physical quantity is temperature that changes from 40 to 80 degrees. As the temperature rises, it passes through every possible fraction of a degree between 40 and 80.

One analog computer with which you are familiar is the mercury thermometer. It measures temperature, which is the degree of hotness of a substance. Hotness is the average energy of molecules that make up the substance. It would be impossible to measure directly the energy of billions of molecules. But molecules radiate, or send out, energy in the form of heat waves. The hotter the substance, the more heat waves it radiates in a unit of time. If the heat waves pass through the glass bulb of a thermometer (Fig. 24), the mercury in the bulb absorbs them. This increases the energy of the mercury molecules, causing them to move faster and increasing the average distance separating them. This, in turn, causes the mercury to expand and rise in the tube above the bulb. The column of mercury will rise until the average energy of the mercury molecules equals the average energy of those of the substance that is having its temperature measured. For example, if the thermometer bulb is in hot water, the mercury will rise until the average energy of the mercury molecules equals the average energy of the water molecules. From these facts, you can see that the length of the column is directly proportional to the average energy—the temperature—of the water molecules. So, the increase or decrease of the length of the mercury column is an analog of the increase or decrease of temperature.

In the thermometer-computer, the input is the energy absorbed by the mercury, and the output is the length of the mercury column which is read on a scale marked in divisions that represent degrees of temperature. (See also THERMOMETER in this book.)

A speedometer (Fig. 24) is another kind of analog computer. Its input is the number of turns of the wheels of an automobile, motorcycle, bicycle, or other vehicle, in a unit of time. The speedometer changes this input to output in the form of a pointer moving across a scale that indicates miles per hour. The distances the pointer moves are analogs of the changes in speed of the vehicle.

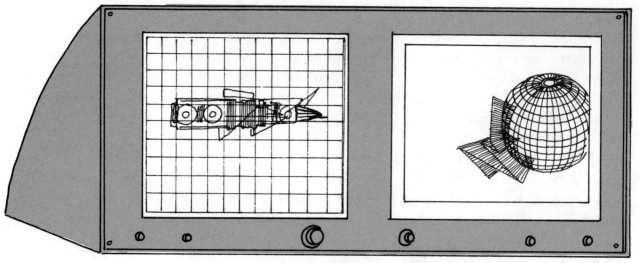

ANALOG COMPUTER VISUAL DISPLAY OUTPUT

FIGURE 25

All of the analog computers we have just described are mechanical devices, but there are electronic analog computers, too. These are equation-solving instruments. Physical processes and events can be described by mathematical equations. The equations are mathematical analogs of the processes and events. For example, the equation that is the analog of a moving object is *rate equals distance divided by time*, or $r = \dfrac{d \text{ (distance)}}{t \text{ (time)}}$

As an object moves, distance and time change continuously. The computer needs input data which are continuous measurements of distance and time, so that numbers can be substituted for the letters d and t in the equation. These are obtained by measuring the distance the object moves in a unit of time. The measurements are collected by *sensors*, devices which respond to changes in physical quantities such as sound, heat, light, time, acceleration, and others. A microphone is a sound sensor and a photoelectric cell is a light sensor. The sensors used in electronic analog computers change the measurements of physical quantities into proportionate amounts of electric current. A distance-measuring sensor might be a wheel rolling along a road or a receiver of radar waves. Time sensors are clocks or any other devices that divide time into equal lengths.

The electrical impulses from the distance- and time-measuring sensors go to electronic circuits within the computer. These circuits can direct the electrical impulses so that they perform mathematical processes such as addition, subtraction, and much more complicated ones. The circuits are analogs of these processes.

42

The output of an electronic analog computer may be in the form of printed numbers, which are solutions to the equations. Or, the equations may have their solutions as two- or three-dimensional figures (Fig. 25) projected upon the screen of an electron tube, much like the picture tube of a television set.

When *Skylab II* was fired into orbit, sensors aboard the spacecraft collected and broadcast to earth a continuous stream of data concerning *Skylab*'s speed and the direction in which it was moving. Analog computers at the mission-control section of the Houston, Texas, Manned

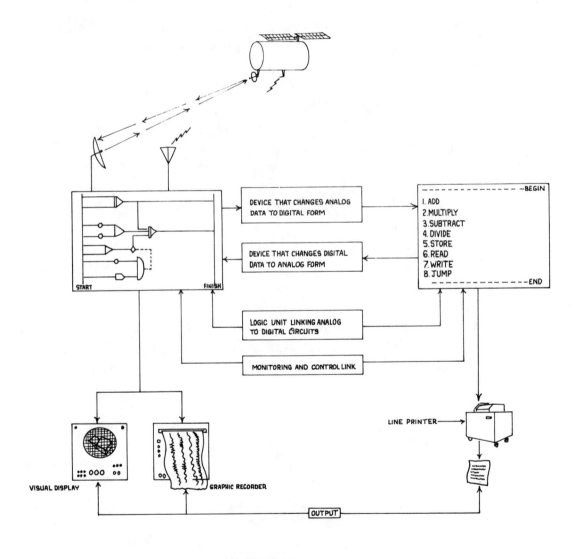

FIGURE 26

Spacecraft Center solved equations that told flight controllers precisely the direction, angle, power, and exact moment a rocket would have to be fired to boost a spacecraft carrying three astronauts to a rendezvous with the orbiting laboratory.

All analog computers answer the question, "How much?"—how much temperature, length, weight, speed, power, and other continuously changing physical quantities. Analog computers are not as accurate as digital computers. Very often, electronic analog computers are used in conjunction with digital computers (Fig. 26).

DIGITAL COMPUTERS

Digital computers are calculating machines that count and then answer the question, "How many?" When most people refer to computers, they mean electronic digital computers; however, there are nonelectronic digital computers, as well. One of the latter kind with which you are familiar is a cash register. The input data of a cash register are the prices (*how many* dollars and cents) of the items bought. The output is the sum of the prices, which is printed on a slip of paper.

A digital computer gets its name from the fact that it works with digits, which are the numbers from 0 to 9. Unlike a continuously changing physical quantity, each number is an unchanging quantity that is separate from other numbers.

Some nonelectronic digital computers, such as calculators and comptometers, can perform all the operations of arithmetic: addition, subtraction, multiplication, and division. These machines, as well as adding machines and cash registers, use the *decimal* system of numbers, which is based on calculation by units and tens. Although each of these machines works in a different manner, all use similar arrangements of gears (Fig. 27). The gear that represents the 1's position in arithmetic can make 10

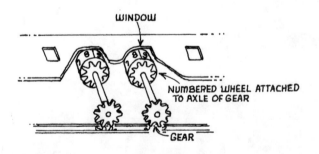

FIGURE 27

stops (representing the digits 0 to 9) as it completes one full turn. The next gear to the left represents the 10's position in arithmetic, and the gear next left is the 100's gear. This series continues through the 1,000's, 100,000's, and 1,000,000's positions. By causing each gear to make the proper number of turns, a series of seven gears can be made to represent any number from 1 to 1,000,000. Larger numbers simply require more gears.

An electronic digital computer can perform all the operations that nonelectronic computers can. It also compares numbers to determine whether they are equal, or which is larger, and it makes many other decisions of this kind. It can very quickly pick out one or a few pieces of data from vast amounts of data.

THE ELECTRONIC COMPUTER SYSTEM

If you were to walk into a room in which a large electronic computer is at work, it might well look like Figure 28. You would see that a computer is a *system* of several parts working together. The diagram below the illustration shows how the parts are related to each other. Each part is called a *unit*. The five main units are *input*, *control*, *storage* (or *memory*), *arithmetic* (or *logic*), and *output*. The random access storage also is a part of the computer system.

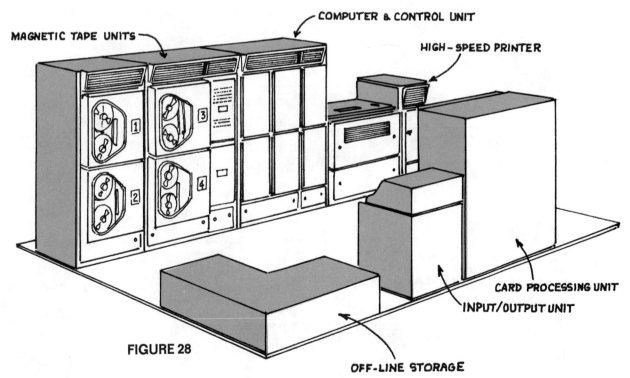

FIGURE 28

INPUT UNIT

The input unit puts data into the control unit or the storage unit. (Fig. 29.) Six input devices are shown in the diagram. As data from an input device moves through the input unit, it is read and changed to a form that the rest of the computer can use. For example, decimal numbers punched into cards are changed to binary numbers.

PUNCHED CARDS. The letters, as well as the numbers, on punched cards are changed from the decimal to the binary system.

PAPER TAPE. Paper tape may contain five or eight *channels*, or rows, of circular punched holes in columns (Fig. 29) . The punches are put into the tape according to a code that can be read as letters and numbers. The code is similar to the one used for punched cards.

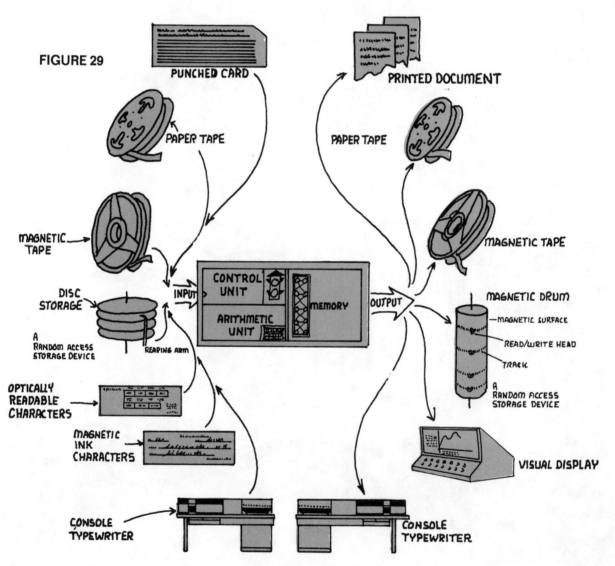

FIGURE 29

PUNCHED CARD

PRINTED DOCUMENT

PAPER TAPE

PAPER TAPE

MAGNETIC TAPE

MAGNETIC TAPE

MAGNETIC DRUM

— MAGNETIC SURFACE

— READ/WRITE HEAD

— TRACK

DISC STORAGE

INPUT

CONTROL UNIT

MEMORY

OUTPUT

ARITHMETIC UNIT

A RANDOM ACCESS STORAGE DEVICE

READING ARM

A RANDOM ACCESS STORAGE DEVICE

OPTICALLY READABLE CHARACTERS

MAGNETIC INK CHARACTERS

VISUAL DISPLAY

CONSOLE TYPEWRITER

CONSOLE TYPEWRITER

MAGNETIC TAPE. The magnetic tape used in computers is much like the tape used in sound recorders, but it is usually of better quality and is twice as wide. The tape is made of a thin plastic ribbon coated with *magnetic iron oxide,* a substance that can be magnetized very easily. As the tape passes over a *read-write head* (Fig. 29), it is exposed to a magnetic field that continually varies in strength from very strong to zero. The changing strength of the magnetic field is due to the changing strength of an electric current that is passing through the read-write head. The changing current may come from a punched-card reader, an optical character reader, or a magnetic-ink character reader. Finally, the continually changing magnetic field magnetizes the iron-oxide in a pattern that reproduces the changes in electric current. The magnetic read-write head thereby "writes" on the magnetic tape the data that was read electrically by the readers. When the tape is used as input for a computer, the data on the tape is read by the input unit and transmitted to the proper place in the computer system.

OPTICALLY READABLE CHARACTERS AND MAGNETIC-INK CHARACTERS. These bits of data may or may not be recorded upon a tape before being put into the computer. They need not be put on the tape because they can be read directly into the system.

RANDOM ACCESS STORAGE. Much data is stored in punched card files and reels of magnetic tape. To have such data quickly available for use in a computer can be a problem. Suppose you have a list of, say, 50,000 people, plus data about each individual. You want to get data that goes with a name beginning with A, and then a name beginning with Z, the next name you want begins with D, and the next with U. You don't know each of the latter three names until you have found the one before it. You would have to sort almost all the way from one end of the card file to the other, and the process might take half an hour. Or you would have to run a tape reel from beginning to end, back to the beginning, and then to the end. All of this would slow down the operation of a computer into which you wanted to put the data. *Random access devices* store data in a form that makes it easy and quick to find. One of these devices is the *disc file* (Fig. 29). Each disc contains data in circles called *records.* A read-write head is positioned above each disc. The arrangement makes it possible to obtain a piece of data from a disc in 1/200 of a second.

CONSOLE KEYBOARD. This device is a keyboard that enables an operator to put data into a computer at any place desired in the storage unit.

STORAGE UNIT

The storage unit holds data that comes to it from (1) input, (2) the arithmetic unit, and (3) the control unit. The storage unit is also called the *memory*. It sends out data to the arithmetic unit and to the output unit. The storage unit is used mainly to hold information needed for the solution of particular problems, or a series of problems of the same kind, and information worked out by the arithmetic unit. Very large amounts of data are stored in punched cards, tape reels, and random access devices outside the computer system.

CONTROL UNIT

The control unit directs the working of all other units of the computer. Its operation is decided by people who present the control unit with the kind of problem they want solved, the kind of answer desired, and the procedure it must follow for getting the answer. This unit makes decisions such as more or less, equal or unequal, yes or no, true or false.

Suppose your bank wants to know the amount of money in your account after one of your checks comes in for payment. The bank instructs its computer to subtract the amount of the check from the amount of money left in your account after your last check was paid. Then the bank would instruct the control unit to find out whether the remainder is less than zero (meaning that your account is overdrawn), zero (no money left in your account), or more than zero (money left in your account).

ARITHMETIC UNIT

The control unit transmits to the arithmetic unit bits of data from the memory unit or from input. As the data enters the arithmetic unit, it is held in temporary storage devices called *registers*. Data is then taken out of the registers as the arithmetic unit works on the problem. As parts of the answer are received, they are stored in other registers. As each main section of the problem is solved, the control unit takes the answer out of the registers and sends it to storage or output.

OUTPUT UNIT

The output unit receives processed data from the control unit and sends it, in the form of electrical impulses, to output devices. These can (1) punch the information into cards or paper tape, (2) record it on magnetic tape, (3) record it in random access devices, (4) make a visual display, which may be lighted numbers or letters on a screen, or (5) print a report with a high-speed printer.

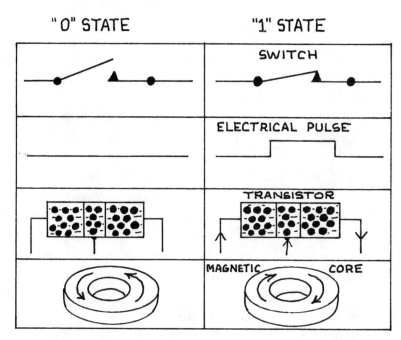

FIGURE 30

THE BINARY NUMBER SYSTEM

Since an electronic computer has no moving parts, it cannot make use of mechanical devices such as wheels with numbers on their rims, as adding machines do. The computer has to represent numbers by means of something that electric current can do. It can flow or not flow. It can flow through a wire in one direction or in the opposite direction. If there were a number of switches in a computer, current would flow when a switch is closed and not flow when a switch is open (Fig. 30). A single pulse of electric current might indicate something and no pulse could indicate the opposite. Current might cause electrons to be emitted across an electrical barrier in a transistor, and no current would mean no electron emission. Electric current could magnetize a small ring, or core, so that the lines of magnetic force go around either clockwise or counterclockwise. With only two states in which switches, transistors, or magnetic cores can exist, a digital electronic computer is limited to using just two numbers. The two are 0 and 1. The 0 is represented by an open switch, no pulse of electric current, no electron emission in a transistor, or lines of magnetic force going around a core counterclockwise. The 1, then, is represented by a closed switch, electron emission, or clockwise lines of magnetic force. In computers, the 1 and 0 are known as the "on" and "off" states. The computer must use a system of arithmetic and logic based on the digits 1 and 0. Such a system is the *binary number system*.

DECIMAL NUMBER SYSTEM

Before we can understand the binary system, we must be sure we understand the decimal system. This is the number system we ordinarily use. It is based on 10 numbers, or *digits:* 0, 1, 2, 3, 4, 5, 6, 7, 8, and 9. All other numbers are made up of combinations of these ten digits. In all numbers greater than 10, the *position* of a digit decides the value of the number. The rightmost position is called the *units* position. The next position to the left is the *tens*, then the *hundreds*, then the *thousands*, and so on. Only one of the digits from 0 to 9 may be in any one position. In writing the number 123, for example, you write a 1 in the hundreds position, a 2 in the tens position, and a 3 in the units position. You have written a number equal to the sum of one *hundred*, two *tens*, and three *units*, or *ones*.

If you want to multiply any digit by itself, you can indicate this by writing the digit and a small number above and to the right of the digit. The small number, called an *exponent*, tells how many times you want to multiply the digit by itself. For example, 2^2 means 2×2; 3^4 means $3 \times 3 \times 3 \times 3$. Any digit with a 0 exponent is equal to 1. A digit with an exponent is called an *exponential*. Look at this table:

10,000	1,000	100	10	1
(ten thousands)	(thousands)	(hundreds)	(tens)	(units)
10^4	10^3	10^2	10^1	10^0
8	5	0	4	6

The decimal number written above is 85,046. Another way of writing this number is

$$
\begin{aligned}
8 \times 10^4 &= 8 \times 10,000 = 80,000 \\
5 \times 10^3 &= 5 \times 1,000 = 5,000 \\
0 \times 10^2 &= 0 \times 100 = 000 \\
4 \times 10^1 &= 4 \times 10 = 40 \\
6 \times 10^0 &= 6 \times 1 = 6 \\
\hline
\text{Sum} && 85,046
\end{aligned}
$$

In these numbers, the 10 is called the *base*. By writing 10 with the proper exponent, you can write any number. Indeed, it is not necessary to use 10 as a base. Any digit except 0 and 1 could be used. We cannot use 0 because 0 multiplied by itself any number of times is still equal to

0. And 1 with any exponent remains equal to 1. The scientists who developed computers chose 2 as the base for computer arithmetic.

Examine this table:

2^7	2^6	2^5	2^4	2^3	2^2	2^1	2^0	—exponential form
128	64	32	16	8	4	2	1	—position value

Now, let us write the number 211, using the base 2.

$$1 \times 2^7 = 1 \times (2 \times 2 \times 2 \times 2 \times 2 \times 2 \times 2) = 128$$
$$1 \times 2^6 = 1 \times (2 \times 2 \times 2 \times 2 \times 2 \times 2) \times = 64$$
$$0 \times 2^5 = 0 \times (2 \times 2 \times 2 \times 2 \times 2) = 0$$
$$1 \times 2^4 = 1 \times (2 \times 2 \times 2 \times 2) = 16$$
$$0 \times 2^3 = 0 \times (2 \times 2 \times 2) = 0$$
$$0 \times 2^2 = 0 \times (2 \times 2) = 0$$
$$1 \times 2^1 = 1 \times (2) = 2$$
$$1 \times 2^0 = 1 \times (1) = 1$$
$$\overline{211}$$

If you look at the leftmost column, you will see another way to write 211:

2^7	2^6	2^5	2^4	2^3	2^2	2^1	2^0	—exponential form
1	1	0	1	0	0	1	1	—position

The lower line is 211 written in binary form. The 1 means that 211 includes the value of the exponential in the position the 1 appears. The 0 means that 211 does not include the exponential in that position.

Let us write a few more numbers in binary form:

BINARY	DECIMAL
0	0
$1 = 2^0$	1
$10 = 2^1 + 0$	2
$11 = 2^1 + 2^0$	3
$100 = 2^2 + 0^1 + 0^0$	4
$101 = 2^2 + 0^1 + 2^0$	5
$110 = 2^2 + 2^1 + 0^0$	6
$111 = 2^2 + 2^1 + 2^0$	7
$1000 = 2^3 + 0^2 + 0^1 + 0^0$	8
$1001 = 2^3 + 0^2 + 0^1 + 2^0$	9
$1010 = 2^3 + 0^2 + 2^1 + 2^0$	10
$1111 = 2^3 + 2^2 + 2^1 + 2^0$	15
$11101 = 2^4 + 2^3 + 2^2 + 0^0 + 2^0$	29
$1011000 = 2^6 + 0^5 + 2^4 + 2^3 + 0^2 + 0^{11} + 0^0$	88

Seeing how any number can be represented by 1's and 0's makes clear how the electrical *on* and *off* states (Fig. 31) in a computer can represent numbers.

The smallest unit of data that can be stored in a computer is a *bit*. This word is a contraction of the words "binary di*git*." A bit is represented in a computer by an "on" or an "off" state. Because of this fact, the on/off states are sometimes called bit/no bit states. A certain number of bits make up a *character*, which may be a number, a letter, or a special character such as &, $, #, ?, and others. A character occupies one storage position, or *frame*. Characters are grouped into *words*. A word is any number made up of bits, for example, 11101. A word also is an actual word or an abbreviation in any language. And certain special characters such as @ and &. Words may be organized into *records*, and records into *files*.

BINARY CODED DECIMALS

If you compare the decimal number 211 with its binary form, 1101011, you will see how much easier and more convenient it is to write the decimal. It would be nice to be able to combine the decimal form with the on/off way of indicating binary numbers. This is what computer scientists did when they created the *binary coded decimal* (BCD) system. It arranges certain decimal digits in a column which makes it possible for them to be represented by on/off states or binary digits. The column is

```
0   8
0   4
●   2
0   1
```

The zeros before each digit represent memory cores in the computer. A filled-in zero represents the "on" state, and an empty zero the "off" state. The column makes up one frame. In the frame above, the number represented is 2 because the core in the 2 position is "on." If more than one core is in the "on" state, the frame has the value of the sum of all the "on" positions. The digits 0 through 9 in the binary coded decimal system have these on/off states:

8	0	0	0	0	0	0	0	0	●	●
4	0	0	0	0	●	●	●	●	0	0
2	0	0	●	●	0	0	●	●	0	0
1	0	●	0	●	0	●	0	●	0	●
	0	1	2	3	4	5	6	7	8	9

If we substitute 1 for the "on" state and 0 for the "off" state, the digits 0 through 9 in the binary coded decimal system become:

```
8   0   0   0   0   0   0   0   0   1   1
4   0   0   0   0   1   1   1   1   0   0
2   0   0   1   1   0   0   1   1   0   0
1   0   1   0   1   0   1   0   1   0   1
   ───────────────────────────────────────
    0   1   2   3   4   5   6   7   8   9
```

Finally, if we turn the columns on their sides, we can write the ten digits in the binary coded decimal system as

```
0000  0001  0010  0011  0100  0101  0110  0111  1000  1001
  0     1     2     3     4     5     6     7     8     9
```

THE SEVEN-BIT ALPHAMERIC BCD CODE

If we add two more positions and a "check bit" to the BCD system, we get the bits necessary for forming the *Seven-Bit Alphameric BCD Code*, in which we can represent both numbers and letters.

CHECK BIT	ZONE BITS		NUMERIC BITS			
P	B	A	8	4	2	1

FIGURE 31

The zone bits are used almost as they are in punched cards. B and A together substitute for the 12 zone, B for the 11 zone, and A for the 0 zone. For example,

LETTER	F	M	T
Six Bit BCD	110110	100100	010011
Alphameric equivalent	B	B	0
	A	0	A
	0	0	0
	4	4	0
	2	0	2
	0	0	1
	or	or	or
	BA-6	B-4	A-3
Punched Card	12-6	11-4	0-3

53

The following table compares the letters of the alphabet and the digits 0 to 9 in the punched card code and the 7-bit BCD code.

PRINTS AS	DEFINED CHARACTER	CARD CODE	BCD CODE
	BLANK		C
A	A	12-1	B A 1
B	B	12-2	B A 2
C	C	12-3	C B A 21
D	D	12-4	B A 4
E	E	12-5	C B A 4 1
F	F	12-6	C B A 42
G	G	12-7	B A 421
H	H	12-8	B A 8
I	I	12-9	C B A 8 1
—	! (Minus Zero)	11-0	B 8 2
J	J	11-1	C B 1
K	K	11-2	C B 2
L	L	11-3	B 21
M	M	11-4	C B 4
N	N	11-5	B 4 1
O	O	11-6	B 42
P	P	11-7	C B 421
Q	Q	11-8	C B 8
R	R	11-9	B 8 1
‡	‡ Record Mark	0-2-8	A 8 2
S	S	0-2	C A 2
T	T	0-3	A 21
U	U	0-4	C A 4
V	V	0-5	A 4 1
W	W	0-6	A 42
X	X	0-7	C A 421
Y	Y	0-8	C A 8
Z	Z	0-9	A 8 1
0	0	0	C 8 2
1	1	1	1
2	2	2	2
3	3	3	C 21
4	4	4	4
5	5	5	C 4 1
6	6	6	C 42
7	7	7	421
8	8	8	8
9	9	9	C 8 1

The *check bit*, which appears in Figure 31, is also called the *parity bit*. It is put into each frame as a way of having the computer continually check itself for accuracy. The parity bit is put into the frame automatically; the computer operator need not do anything to have it appear in the frame. There are two kinds of parity: even and odd. Even parity means that the total number of bits in any frame must always equal an even number, and odd parity means that the number of bits must be odd. If a code calls for odd parity and, after the check bit has been added, a frame has an even number of bits, the computer signals that an error has been made. The failure of a frame to have proper parity means that a bit was accidentally dropped or added. The parity check is not foolproof. If two bits were dropped or added, parity would be preserved, yet there would be an error in that frame. However, the chance of two bits being added or dropped in the same frame is so small that it is not worth worrying about.

THE WORKING PARTS OF A COMPUTER

A fairly large computer that was taught to play chess had 44,000 transistors, 5,700 diodes, 1,152,000 magnetic memory cores, and 66,500 other electrical units, plus the wires that connected all these parts together. The magnetic cores store data, and the diodes and transistors do the arithmetic and make possible the control activities.

Transistors and diodes act as electronic switches. They work at extreme speeds. A high-speed switching transistor can open and close in a few billionths of a second. Transistors are also used to store numbers for a short time. For example, to hold the augend and addend bits during addition.

DIODES. A diode is a one-way electronic switch. It has no moving parts. Electric current arriving from one direction can pass through the diode. If the current arrives from the other direction, the diode will not let it pass. The diode acts as a one-way current gate. Current passing through a diode may represent the "on" state, or 1 in binary arithmetic. Current blocked from passing through a diode may represent the "off" state, or 0.

Series of diodes can be connected so that they electronically represent logical ideas. For example, the idea of "and" means "both of two things." "A cow *and* a horse" means both the cow and the horse together. This is the idea behind addition. Two plus four (2 + 4) means two and four put together. Suppose we connect two diodes in a circuit as shown in Figure 32. The electric current may enter the circuit through either

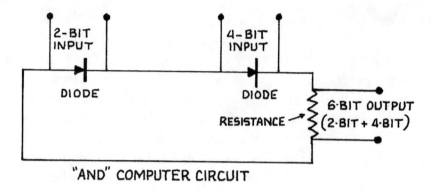

"AND" COMPUTER CIRCUIT

FIGURE 32

diode. The current must flow in the direction of the arrows, because the diodes will not allow it to flow in the opposite direction. The resistance in the circuit is an electrical device that holds back the free flow of current. If current representing the 2-bit enters the circuit, it is not strong enough to flow through the resistance. If current from the 4-bit is added, then we have a 2-bit current *and* 4-bit current. The current is now strong enough to pass through the resistance and leave the circuit as output. So, the diode circuit added 2 and 4. Diodes can be used in other circuits to represent ideas such as "this one or that one or both," "at least one of such-and-such a number," and others.

TRANSISTORS. We may think of a transistor as being two diodes connected back-to-back plus a path for current to enter between the two (Fig. 33). Current entering the transistor from A passes through diode d_1, but is blocked by diode d_2, which faces in the direction opposite that of d_1. If a small amount of current is sent through C, however, current can flow through d_2 and the current leaving B is amplified.

Figure 33 shows a transistor circuit that represents the idea "or." If a bit pulse of current enters this circuit through the A input, B input, or C input, it will leave the circuit as output. So, the circuit represents "either A *or* B *or* C."

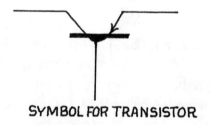

SYMBOL FOR TRANSISTOR

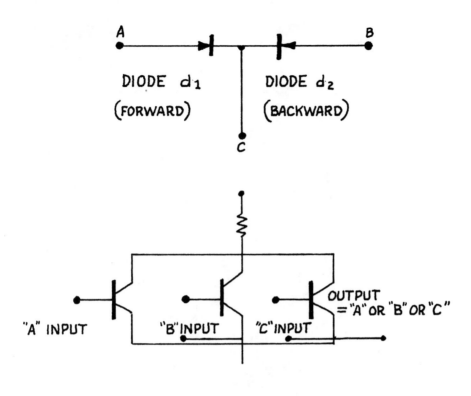

FIGURE 33

Transistors act as *toggle switches* when they are connected into a *flip-flop circuit*. A toggle switch with which you are familiar is the wall electric light switch. You push on it with a certain amount of strength, and then it suddenly flips the rest of the way. If you push it in the opposite direction, it will flop back. If a strong enough current is sent into a transistor in a flip-flop circuit, the transistor suddenly flips and stores a bit. Then, if current of equal strength is sent in the opposite direction, the transistor switch flops and stores the opposite bit. In this way, the transistor can be made to store a 1 bit or a 0 bit. Collections of flip-flop circuits make up the computer's registers. After flipping bits into a register, a transistor flip-flop circuit can be made to flop them out all at once to clear the register.

MEMORY CORES. The storage, or memory, unit of a computer is made up of memory cores. These are very small rings made of iron oxide plus manganese oxide and magnesium oxide. Each ring is only about 75/1000 of an inch in diameter. Hundreds of thousands of them can be arranged, in layers, in less than one cubic foot of space.

57

CLOCKWISE "ON" 1-BIT

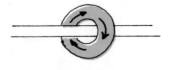

NO CURRENT

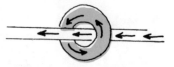

COUNTER-CLOCKWISE "OFF" NO-BIT

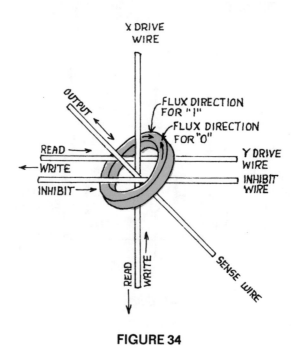

FIGURE 34

A core can be magnetized in either of two states: with the lines of magnetic force running clockwise or with the lines running counterclockwise. The clockwise direction represents the "on" state, or 1. The counterclockwise direction represents the "off" state, or 0. A core is magnetized by passing a current along a wire that runs through the center of the core. A current flowing in one direction magnetizes the core clockwise; a current flowing in the opposite direction magnetizes the core counterclockwise (Fig. 34). The core remains magnetized in the direction given it by the last current to flow through.

Four wires pass through a core and connect it to other cores and other parts of the computer. The X DRIVE WIRE and the Y DRIVE WIRE carry current for magnetizing the core. The words READ at the ends of these wires mean that they are used to call for information stored on cores. This is known as *reading*. The words WRITE mean that, by reversing the direction of the current, information is sent into storage on the same wires. This is called *writing*. The SENSE WIRE enables the control unit to tell whether or not the core is magnetized. This is how

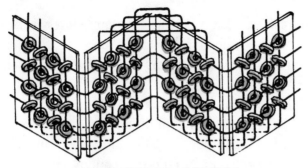

MAGNETIC CORE MEMORY PLANES

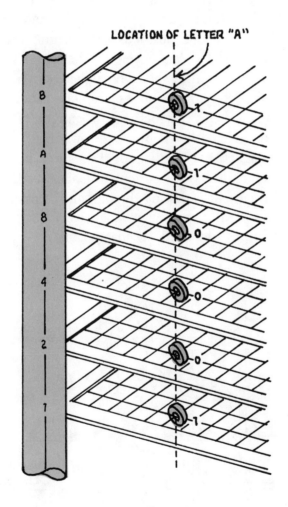

LOCATION OF LETTER "A"

FIGURE 35

the control unit can tell that a core at a certain address is or is not being used to store a bit. And the INHIBIT wire prevents the bit on the core from changing from 1 to 0, or vice versa, when the current changes direction from "read" to "write."

Since a single core stores only one bit of a computer word, a large number of cores are required to contain all the bits in every word to be stored. The cores are mounted on *planes* (Fig. 35), and the planes are stacked one upon another. Each core can contain only one bit of data. A vertical column of cores consisting of one core in each plane is used to store one character. The column is called a *storage position*. The location of each bit in a storage column is the *address* of that bit. The address includes both the column and the row in which the core is located. Any number of neighboring storage positions can be grouped together to form a word. Figure 35 shows one character, the letter A, in a storage position of a computer that is using the six-bit alphameric code.

Figure 36 shows an array of memory cores. The core at the address, *3rd row-4th column*, is being magnetized by current flowing through drive wires in the directions shown by the arrows. Half the amount of current needed to magnetize a core is sent through each wire. The sum of the two half amounts is enough current to magnetize the core. Since only half the needed current is passing through all the other cores in the 3rd row and 4th column, they are not magnetized. In this way, just one core can be picked out, or addressed, for magnetizing.

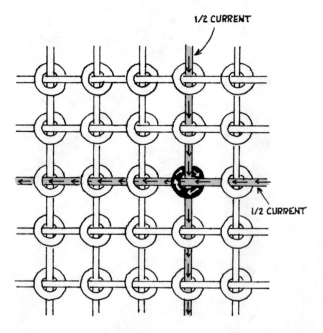

FIGURE 36

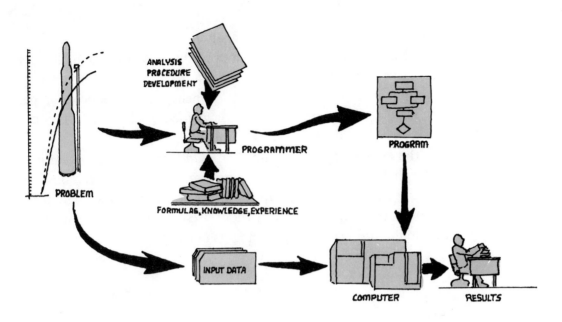

FIGURE 37

PROGRAMMING

We have a data processing problem we want to solve, and we have decided that a computer is to be used. To have the computer solve the problem, we must give it instructions. Giving these instructions is called *programming*. A program usually is long and complex because it is intended to solve difficult problems or problems that have many pieces of data; also, a program usually is long because the instructions must be given in very small steps.

A person who writes programs is a *programmer*. The first thing he does is to get a job description from the scientists, businessmen, engineers, or others who have a data processing problem. The job description tells exactly what the problem is, what the input data should be, how the data should be processed, and what the form of the answer should be. The programmer may want first to take the problem to a *systems analyst* (Fig. 37), an expert in data processing systems, who may decide that some of the problems might be better solved on data processing machines other than the computer. He will describe a processing system in which all machines are included. Knowing from the system analyst's report just what must be done, the programmer gets ready to write his program.

61

The programmer (or the systems analyst) first makes out a *systems flow chart* (Fig. 38) that indicates the movement of data through all parts of a data processing system. The chart contains symbols for the different kinds of input and output equipment (punched cards, punched tape, magnetic tape, optically readable and magnetic-ink characters, random access devices, line printers, and visual displays).

Next, the programmer makes up a *program flow chart*, or *operations flow chart*, that breaks down the job into operations and decisions the computer must perform. Figure 38 shows an operations flow chart for a small problem that can be solved without a computer, but which shows how a computer proceeds in performing its operations.

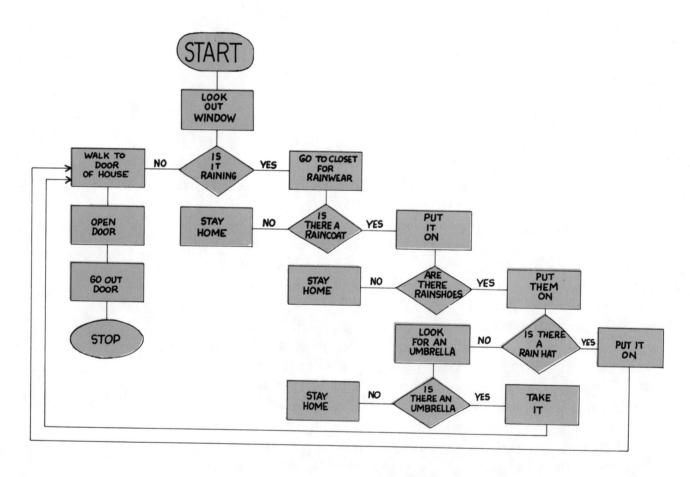

FIGURE 38

The programmer further breaks down the program by writing detailed instructions on printed forms called *coding sheets* (Fig. 39). He also makes out memory maps, which show the addresses of certain pieces of data. He writes in *computer language*. Computer language is a set of abbreviations and the rules by which the abbreviations are put together to form instructions for the computer. There are different languages for different kinds of computers and types of problems. For example, problems that concern the world of business are written in COBOL (COmmon Business Oriented Language). If the problem is mathematical, particularly if it can be solved by algebra, the programmer would use FORTRAN (FORmula TRANslation). An instruction written in FORTRAN might read, DO 7 L = 1, 25. This instructs the computer, "Repeat the next 7 operations while a counter L goes from 1 to 25, increasing in steps of 1; when L passes 25, stop." Or, in IBM/360 language, T 5, R SUM means "load the contents of SUM R in register 5."

When the program is coded, the programmer has the instructions put on one or more kinds of input devices. For example, he may have the instructions punched onto cards. The cards are then placed into an input device that translates the punches into machine language, which is in the binary system.

When the program has been stored in the computer, the programmer puts into the computer the data of a problem for which he knows the answer. If the program does not produce this answer—and it usually does not—the program has flaws, or *bugs*. The programmer must then work to get the flaws out, or *debug* the program. In doing this work, he controls the computer from a console with control buttons.

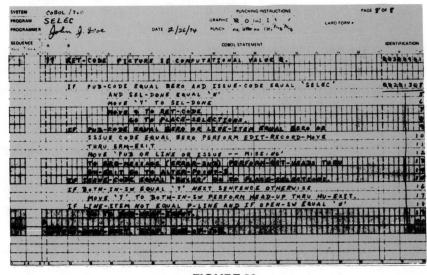

FIGURE 39

FAMILIAR THINGS

SEWING MACHINES

A sewing machine sews neater and faster than you can sew by hand. It also sews in a different way. Ordinary hand stitches are made by using a needle to pull thread through cloth, first in one direction and then in the opposite direction. This kind of in-and-out weaving action makes the simplest kind of stitch, a *plainstitch* (Fig. 40-A). In plainstitching, the whole needle goes through the cloth, being first on one side and then on the other. A sewing machine needle is attached to the machine, so it must remain on one side of the cloth. Thus, a sewing machine cannot make plainstitches. The simplest machine-made stitch is the *single-thread stitch*, or *chainstitch*. This kind of stitch is often found in clothing sewn by machines in clothing factories. A chainstitch appears as a straight line of thread on the top surface of the cloth and a series of interlocked loops on the underside (Fig. 40-B). You can unravel a chainstitch by pulling on one end of the thread.

The most common sewing machine stitch is the *double-thread stitch* or *lockstitch* (Fig. 40-C). This is the stitch most often made by home sewing machines. A lockstitch appears as a straight line on both sides of the cloth. You cannot unravel a lockstitch by pulling on one end of the thread.

64

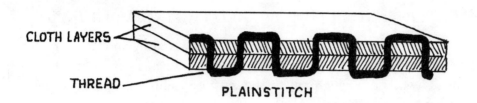

CLOTH LAYERS

THREAD

PLAINSTITCH

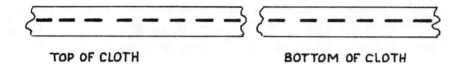

TOP OF CLOTH

BOTTOM OF CLOTH

FIGURE 40-A

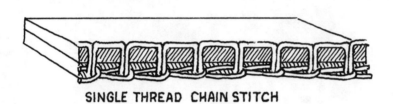

SINGLE THREAD CHAIN STITCH

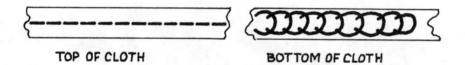

TOP OF CLOTH

BOTTOM OF CLOTH

FIGURE 40-B

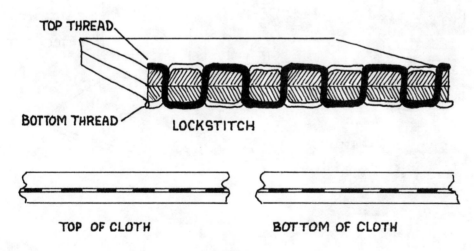

TOP THREAD

BOTTOM THREAD

LOCKSTITCH

TOP OF CLOTH

BOTTOM OF CLOTH

FIGURE 40-C

ELECTRIC- AND FOOT-POWERED SEWING MACHINES

A modern sewing machine (Fig. 41) is powered by an electric motor. The motor is connected by a belt or a chain to a main shaft within the machine. The other moving parts of the sewing machine are driven by gears attached to the main shaft. All this machinery is located in the *body, arm,* and *base* of the machine. At one end of the main shaft is a heavy wheel called a *hand wheel.* It increases the momentum of the turning shaft. This means that the hand wheel increases the tendency of the shaft to keep turning. The hand wheel gets its name from the fact that if you want to turn the shaft just once, as you must in certain operations, you can do this by turning the wheel by hand. For example, you turn the hand wheel to raise the needle for threading. The motor is switched on

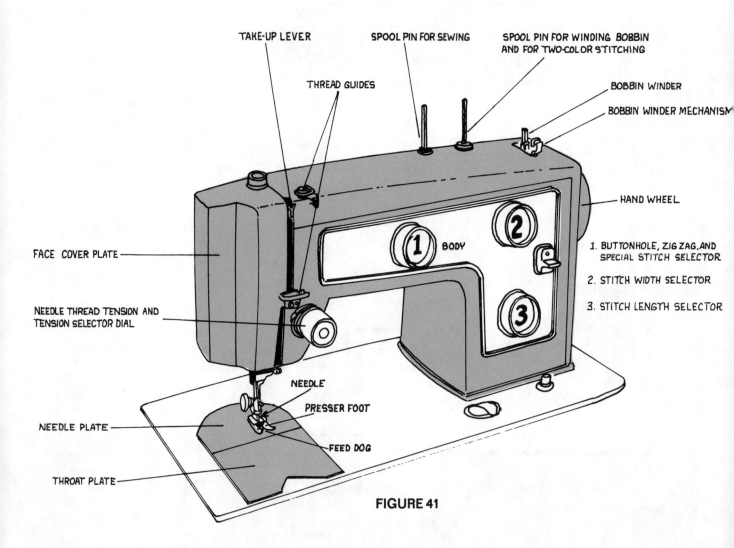

FIGURE 41

and off by a foot pedal or by a lever operated by the sewer's knee. Old-fashioned sewing machines and those for use where there is no electric power are set in motion by a foot-operated treadle.

THE BOBBIN

Before sewing begins, thread is unwound from the spool on which it is wound when it is bought and at the same time is wound on a metal or plastic spool called a *bobbin* (Fig. 42). This is done in slightly different ways on different sewing machines. In general, the spool is put upon a short stationary metal rod called a *spool pin*, or *spool post*. The spool pin goes through the hole in the spool of thread. Some sewing machines have only one spool pin, which is used first for winding the bobbin and then during sewing. Most sewing machines have two spool pins. One is used for winding bobbins and the other for sewing. Near the spool pin is the *bobbin winder*, a round metal rod with a slot in its side at the upper end. Within the slot is a catch attached to a spring. The hole in the bobbin fits over the bobbin winder and the spring pushes the catch into the slot, holding the bobbin tightly.

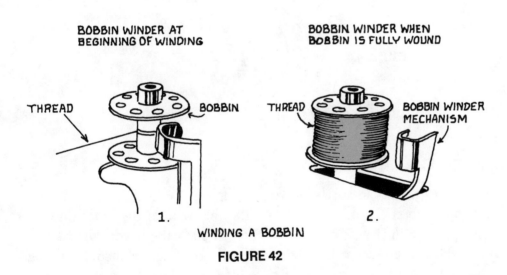

WINDING A BOBBIN

FIGURE 42

The bobbin winder spins very rapidly, pulling thread from the spool and winding it on the bobbin. Next to the bobbin winder is a device called the *bobbin winder mechanism*. The uppermost part of this device fits between the top and bottom of the bobbin (Fig. 43). A spring holds it against the thread that is being wound onto the bobbin. As the coil of thread increases in thickness, the bobbin winder mechanism is pushed outward from the center of the bobbin. When the bobbin is fully wound,

67

the mechanism has been pushed out far enough to cause it to disconnect the bobbin winder from the main shaft. This stops the bobbin winder.

When the bobbin has been wound, the person operating the sewing machine cuts the thread between the spool and the bobbin. Then the bobbin is taken off the bobbin winder and placed in the *bobbin case* (Fig. 43). This is a metal cup that fits into the bobbin housing, or *bobbin chamber*, a hollow in the base of the machine. In the center of the bobbin chamber is a spool pin that passes through the hole in the bobbin. To reach the bobbin chamber, you pull up a metal plate called the *throat plate*, or *hand-hole cover-plate*. Thread from the bobbin will form the bottom thread of the lockstitch.

Adjoining the throat plate is the *needle plate*, which is immovable and contains the *needle hole*. Within slots in the needle plate are the sharp-toothed edges of two metal strips. These make up the *feed dog*, which moves the cloth past the needle when the machine is sewing. Surrounding the needle are two prongs, or *toes*, attached to a metal rod. These make up the *presser foot* (Fig. 42), which presses the cloth down upon the feed dog.

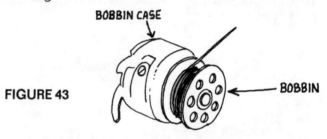

BOBBIN CASE

FIGURE 43

BOBBIN

BOBBIN BEING PUT INTO BOBBIN CASE

MAKING READY TO SEW

After the bobbin has been wound, the top thread must be put into sewing position. To do this, you run the thread from the spool through one or more thick-wire guides and then through the *needle thread tension*. This device keeps the thread properly tight. On a modern sewing machine the needle thread tension includes an adjustable dial to choose the amount of tension needed. The thread then goes through a hole in the *take-up* lever. When the machine is sewing, the take-up lever moves up and down, doing two jobs: as it moves down, it pulls thread from the spool; as it moves up, it tightens stitches. From the take-up lever the thread is run through the eye of the needle. A sewing machine needle has its eye near its point. The thread carried by the needle forms the top thread of the lockstitch.

With the bobbin wound and the needle threaded, you must do two more things before beginning to sew. You turn the hand wheel one full turn and pull on the thread that goes through the eye of the needle. This action pulls the free end of the bobbin thread up through the needle hole. Finally, just before switching on the motor, you lower the presser foot upon the cloth by pulling down a lever that is at the rear of the arm.

SEWING

In the nearly two centuries since the sewing machine was invented, a number of ways to make stitches have been devised. All the different devices make the same kind of stitches in the same way. We will describe only one of these devices, the one that is most common in home sewing machines. It is the *bobbin collar*, a revolving metal hoop that surrounds the bobbin case and has a hook at one point on its upper edge (Fig. 44).

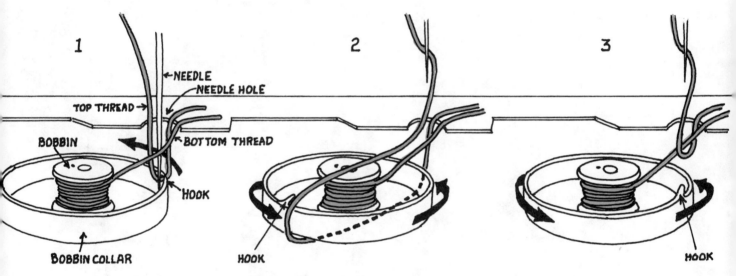

THE SCHEME OF HOW THE NEEDLE AND BOBBIN WORK

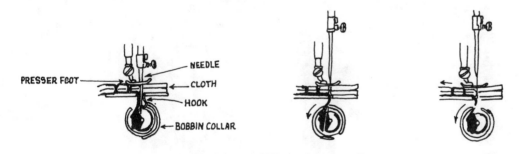

HOW THE WORKING OF THE NEEDLE AND BOBBIN ACTUALLY LOOK

FIGURE 44

69

When the motor is switched on, stitches are made in five steps:

(1) The needle moves down through the cloth and into the needle hole, carrying a loop of thread into the bobbin collar.

(2) When the needle is at its lowest point, the loop of thread is caught by the hook on the bobbin collar. The turning collar pulls the thread over and then under the bobbin case, making a loop. This loop encircles the bobbin case.

(3) As the collar completes a full circle, the hook is again directly beneath the needle hole. Here it casts off the thread.

(4) The needle and take-up lever rise and tighten the loop within the cloth, completing the lockstitch.

(5) When the needle is lifted above the cloth, the feed dog pushes more cloth forward the length of one stitch. Then a new stitch begins.

A modern sewing machine has several controls that enable the sewer to make buttonhole stitches, zigzag stitches (for darning), and a number

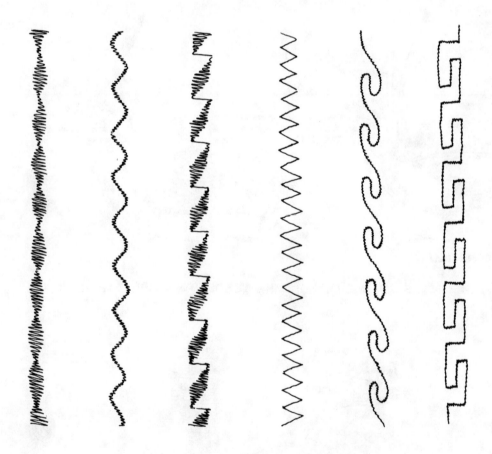

FIGURE 45

of embroidery stitches. Some of these are shown in Fig. 45. Embroidery stitches may be sewn in two colors at once. This requires a *double needle* and two spools of thread of different colors. One spool is put on each of the two spool pins.

SPEEDOMETER and ODOMETER

A *speedometer* tells how *fast* an automobile or other land vehicle is moving. An *odometer* tells how *far* the vehicle has traveled. Every automobile has both a speedometer and an odometer mounted in the dashboard.

Each time a wheel of a car turns once, the car moves a distance equal to the circumference of the tire. If you know the circumference of the tire and the number of times it turns in one minute, you can calculate how fast the car is moving in miles per hour. And if you know how long the car has been traveling, you can figure out how far it has gone. A speedometer and an odometer do these calculations automatically. Each is a kind of computer. (See the section on *Analog Computers* in this book.)

SPEEDOMETER

The first working part of a speedometer is a gear that is fitted around the car's driveshaft (Fig. 46). The driveshaft runs from the engine to the wheels and turns them. The size of the gear depends on the circumference of the tires. It is designed so that when the car is traveling 60 miles per hour, the gear turns 1,000 times per minute. This gear turns a second one. Attached to the second gear is one end of a flexible steel cable. The cable runs into the back of the speedometer in the dashboard.

Attached firmly to the end of the cable in the dashboard is a permanent magnet. The shape of the magnet varies in different speedometers. One kind is a simple bar magnet. An aluminum cup, called a *speedcup,* surrounds the magnet. And a stationary iron cup, called a *field plate,* surrounds the magnet and speedcup. A thin metal shaft runs through the speedcup and is attached firmly to it. One end of this shaft is pointed and the point rests in a hollow in the end of the flexible cable. Attached to the other end of the shaft is a pointer that can turn around a dial on a metal plate. A coil spring on the shaft holds the pointer at zero on the dial when the automobile is not moving. The dial is the one you see through a window in the dashboard.

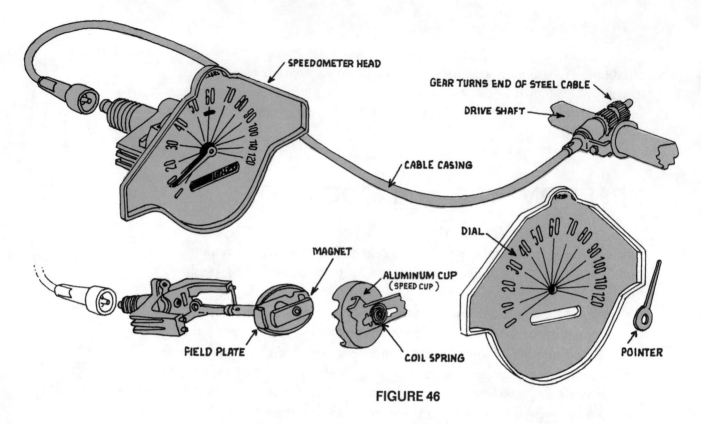

SPEEDOMETER HEAD

GEAR TURNS END OF STEEL CABLE

DRIVE SHAFT

CABLE CASING

DIAL

MAGNET

ALUMINUM CUP
(SPEED CUP)

FIELD PLATE

COIL SPRING

POINTER

FIGURE 46

When the driveshaft turns the car's wheels, it turns the cable, too. This spins the cup-shaped magnet. The spinning magnet causes electric currents, called *eddy currents*, to be produced in the speedcup. The field plate aids in the production of the eddy currents.

These currents cause the aluminum speedcup to act as if it were magnetized. The magnet then pulls the speedcup around in the same direction that the magnet is spinning. Although the magnet is whirling very fast, the speedcup is pulled around less than one complete revolution. The faster the magnet spins, the stronger the eddy currents become and the farther the speedcup turns. The turning cup turns the shaft that is attached to it. The pointer sweeps across the face of the dial. The coil spring balances the force of the turning speedcup, holding the pointer at one place on the dial when the car is moving at a steady speed. When the car moves faster, the magnetic force that moves the speedcup over-balances the force of the spring, and the pointer moves forward. When the car slows, the coil spring overbalances the speedcup, and the pointer moves back.

The spacing between the numbers on the dial is arranged so that every 16.667 turns of the magnet in one minute cause the pointer to move the distance that will indicate one mile per hour of speed. Thus, the speedometer automatically calculates the speed of the car and displays it on the dial in the dashboard. This is how the speedometer acts as a computer.

Instead of a dial, some speedometers have a curved scale of miles that moves past a stationary pointer in a small window. The scale is attached to the aluminum speedcup.

ODOMETER

An odometer consists of five or six numbered wheels, side by side on a shaft (Fig. 47). The wheels are connected to the driveshaft of the automobile by an arrangement of gears and rods. Gears within the numbered wheels are arranged so that when a wheel makes one complete turn, the next wheel to the left makes one-tenth of a turn. The wheels are arranged behind a small window on the dashboard so that only one horizontal row of numbers can be seen through the window.

The gear system is designed so that when the car has traveled one-tenth of a mile, the gear connected directly to the car's driveshaft makes 100 turns. These 100 turns make the gear wheel farthest right move one-tenth of a turn. The number "1" on this wheel shows in the window. One thousand turns of the gear next to the driveshaft cause the odometer wheel to make one full turn. The full turn of this wheel causes the wheel to its left to make one-tenth of a turn, showing that the car has traveled one mile. Following this pattern, one tenth of a turn of the wheel third from the right registers a distance of 10 miles; fourth from the right, 100 miles; fifth, 1000 miles; and sixth, 10,000 miles. On odometers that have only five wheels, the one farthest right registers one-mile distances instead of tenths of a mile. The greatest number of miles an odometer can register is 99,999.9. If you drive one-tenth of a mile more, all the wheels make one-tenth of a turn and register 00000.0. Then the odometer begins to count miles all over again, beginning with one-tenth, although the total mileage is really 100,000.1.

THE ODOMETER

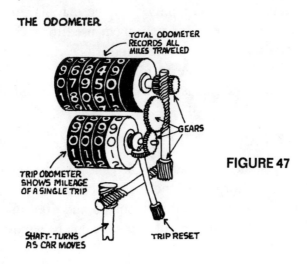

TOTAL ODOMETER RECORDS ALL MILES TRAVELED

GEARS

TRIP ODOMETER SHOWS MILEAGE OF A SINGLE TRIP

SHAFT-TURNS AS CAR MOVES

TRIP RESET

FIGURE 47

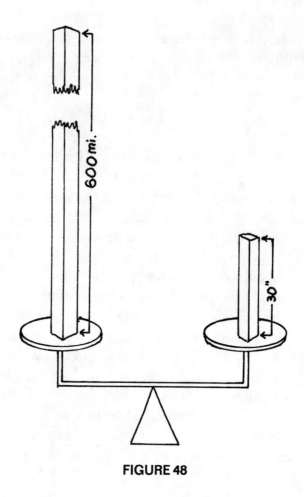

FIGURE 48

BAROMETER

If you have ever listened to a weather forecaster on radio or television, you remember that he probably said something like, "The barometer reads 29.37 inches and is falling." Or, he may have said the barometer was rising. A barometer is an instrument used for measuring the pressure of the air, or atmosphere, that surrounds the earth with an envelope about 600 miles thick. To be able to forecast weather, it's quite important to know what the air pressure is and whether it is rising or falling.

MERCURY BAROMETER

Suppose you had the kind of scale called a balance (Fig. 48) and you could keep all the air out of the space above the pans. Then you put on one pan a column of air one inch square and 600 miles high. It would balance on the other pan a column of mercury almost 30 inches high.

74

(Mercury is the silvery liquid metal you can see in some thermometers.) Each column would weigh 14.7 pounds, or 6.67 kilograms. We can use this fact to make a *mercury barometer*.

We put mercury about two inches deep in a small bowl. We also seal one end of a glass tube a little more than 30 inches long and fill it with mercury. Then, without spilling any mercury, we tip the tube over and place the open end beneath the surface of the mercury in the bowl (Fig. 49). If we hold the tube upright, the column of mercury in the tube will settle to a height of 29.9 inches, or 760 millimeters. The mercury does not run out of the tube because it is held up by the weight of a column of air 600 miles high, which is pushing down with a pressure of 14.7 pounds on every square inch of the surface of the mercury in the dish. All of these measurements are accurate if we are at sea level. Above sea level, the column of air is proportionately shorter. It will weigh less and thus will be balanced by a shorter column of mercury.

If we clamp the glass tube in a vertical position and clamp a yardstick behind it, we will be able to read in fractions of an inch any changes in the height of the column of mercury. The changes will be due to changes in atmospheric pressure.

Although the atmosphere exerts pressure because of its weight, we do not read barometers in units of weight, but in units of length—the length of the mercury column. That's why you hear meteorologists say, "The barometer reads 29.37 inches." Because we use a barometer to measure atmospheric pressure, this pressure is also called *barometric pressure*.

A barometer uses mercury because it is the heaviest liquid. Lighter liquids would make it necessary to have a glass tube too long for convenience. For example, a barometer using water would require a tube at least 34 feet long. French mathematician and philosopher Blaise Pascal made a barometer using wine because red wine is easier to see than colorless water inside a glass tube. Wine being a light liquid, Pascal needed a tube 46 feet long.

Changes in atmospheric pressure are caused by the movement of huge masses of warm air and cold air that continually flow back and forth over the surface of the earth. Warm air is light and cold air is heavy. An area covered by a mass of warm, light air is a *low pressure area*, or simply a "low." And an area covered by cold, heavy air is a *high pressure area*, or a "high." As a high passes over an area, the column of mercury in a barometer is pushed up. It goes down as a low moves into the area, replacing the high. Weather changes with each change in barometric pressure. That is why weather forecasters always talk about highs and lows.

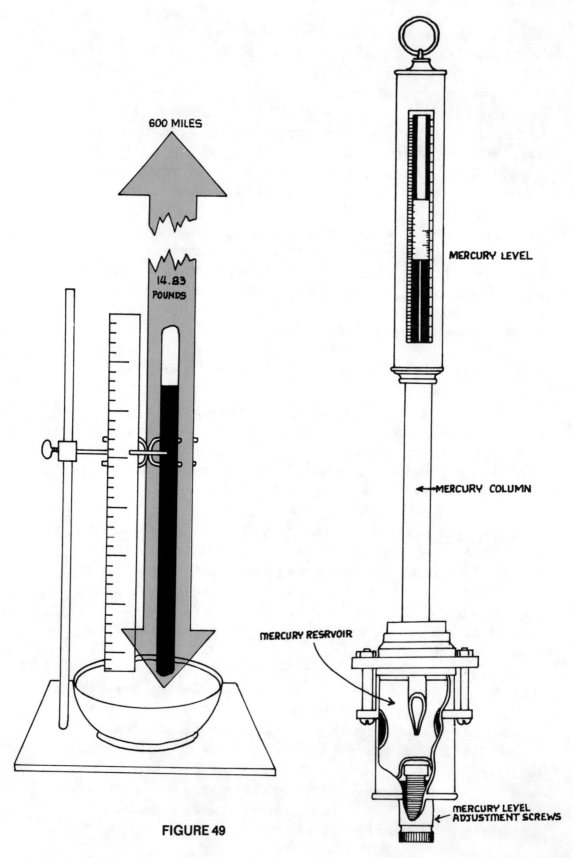

600 MILES

14.83 POUNDS

MERCURY LEVEL

MERCURY COLUMN

MERCURY RESRVOIR

MERCURY LEVEL ADJUSTMENT SCREWS

FIGURE 49

76

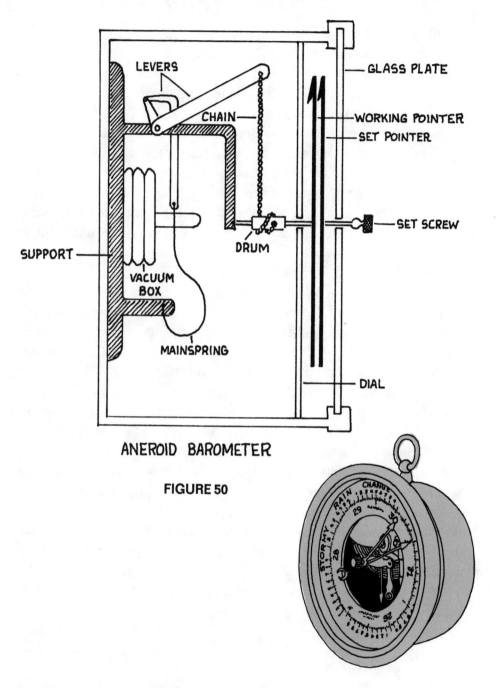

ANEROID BAROMETER

FIGURE 50

ANEROID BAROMETER

There are a number of different kinds of mercury barometers, but all are awkward to handle because of the length of the glass tube. Although a mercury barometer is accurate, it is not very sensitive; it does not show small changes of air pressure very well. A more convenient and sensitive barometer is the *aneroid*. The name means "without liquid." An aneroid barometer consists of an airtight can, called a *vacuum box*, from which most of the air has been pumped. To keep the nearly-15-pounds-per-square-inch pressure of the outside air from crushing the vacuum box, the metal is strengthened by folding it into ridges and grooves. (Fig. 50). The vacuum box is attached to the inside of a container which has holes through which air passes freely.

An increase in air pressure flattens the vacuum box a little. When air pressure decreases, the vacuum box springs back, moving outward a little. The changes in the thickness of the vacuum box are so slight that they would be difficult to see if we tried to observe them directly. To make the slight changes easily visible, a flat spring is attached to the can. The spring transfers the movements of the can to an arrangement of levers that magnify the movements. A chain transfers the movements of the levers to a drum. Attached to the pointer is a lever that moves over a dial on the outside of the barometer. The divisions of the dial represent air pressures equal to inches of mercury in a mercury barometer. When an increase of air pressure moves the can downward, the pointer moves over the dial toward the high-pressure side; a decrease in pressure causes the pointer to move in the opposite direction.

You may want to know whether the pressure has risen or fallen since you last looked at your barometer. To enable you to learn this, an aneroid barometer has a second pointer in front of its dial. This pointer, called the *set pointer*, is attached to a small knob that you can turn with your fingers. The knob sticks out through a hole in the pane of glass that protects the dial. The set pointer is moved until it is directly over the pressure-indicating pointer. As air pressure changes, the indicating pointer moves away from the set pointer toward either the high or low ends of the dial. By noting in which direction the pointer has moved, you can tell whether air pressure rose or fell. Although the set pointer can tell you whether the pressure changed to higher or lower, it cannot disclose whether more than one pressure change has taken place since the last reading. For example, you may find that the barometer shows a pressure lower than when you last saw it, but the pressure may have risen first before it fell.

BAROGRAPH

You can have a complete record of changes in barometric pressure over a period of time if you use a *barograph*. In this instrument, the pointer of an aneroid barometer is replaced by a pen with an automatic ink supply. The pen writes on a long sheet of graph paper that is fastened to a cylinder. (Some barographs use a circular sheet of graph paper fastened to a disc.) Vertical lines printed on the paper represent hours and minutes, and horizontal lines indicate hundredths of an inch of atmospheric pressure. Clockwork causes the cylinder to make one complete turn in 24 hours. The line that the pen draws is an uninterrupted record of rising and falling air pressure for one whole day.

ALTIMETER

For every 900 feet that you carry a barometer above sea level, it will read one inch less. As you ascend, the column of air above becomes shorter; it thus becomes lighter and exerts less pressure. These facts have been used to create an instrument—an *altimeter*—that measures altitude, the distance above sea level. Scientists have agreed that a barometric reading of 29.97 inches, or 760 millimeters, shall be zero altitude, or sea level.

In place of the dial of an aneroid barometer, which reads in inches or millimeters, an altimeter dial reads in feet or meters above sea level. Instead of a dial, some altimeters have a little window in which an airplane pilot sees numbers in the same way you see miles per hour in some automobile speedometers. In one kind of altimeter there are three pointers (Fig. 51). Each is attached to a shaft and each shaft runs through a

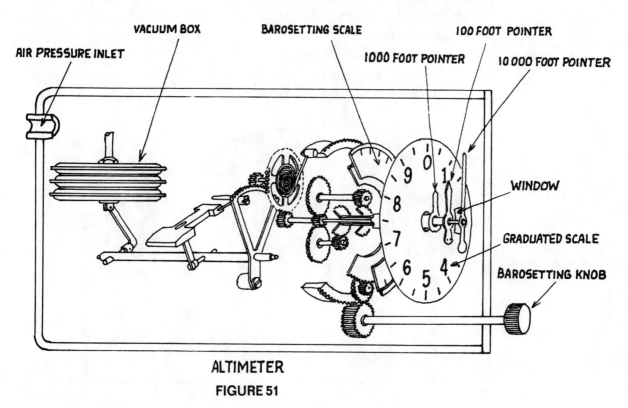

ALTIMETER

FIGURE 51

gear of a different size. The gears are turned by another gear which is attached to the shaft that runs through the drum. The pointer with the smallest gear moves farthest across the dial for any change in air pressure. A pilot watching this pointer reads each division on the dial as 100 feet of altitude. The pointer with the next larger gear moves one-tenth as far as the first pointer for an equal change in altitude. A pilot reading this pointer reads each division on the dial as 1,000 feet of altitude. He reads the pointer attached to the largest gear as showing 10,000-foot changes in altitude.

The reading of an altimeter depends not only on the height of an airplane above sea level, but also on the atmospheric pressure of the area through which the plane is flying. A pilot flying long distances must check with airports along his route to learn of changes in atmospheric pressure. When he receives a report on the pressure, he can adjust his altimeter by turning a small knob on the front of the dial: the *barosetting* knob.

The air-pressure altimeter does not always give the true distance of the plane above the earth's surface. It tells how high above *sea level* a plane is flying, but not necessarily how high above the *ground* (Fig. 52). This is all right for planes flying over oceans, but may cause trouble for those flying over land, especially in mountainous country. An air-pressure altimeter may inform a pilot that his plane has an altitude of 3,000 feet above sea level, but the plane may be flying only 20 feet above a 2,980-foot-high mountain, or perhaps 150 feet below a peak into which the plane may crash. Also, in mountainous country, air pressure is continually being changed by strong upward and downward currents of air. The altimeter of a plane flying in a strong down-current may tell the pilot that his plane

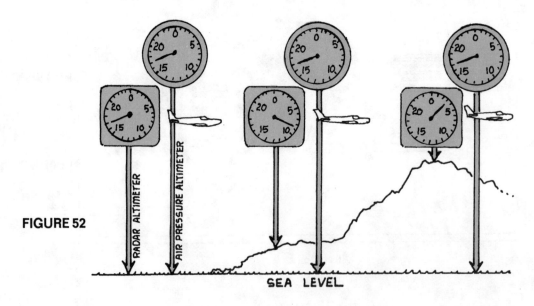

FIGURE 52

RADAR ALTIMETER   AIR PRESSURE ALTIMETER

SEA LEVEL

80

is higher than it actually is, because the down-current increases pressure on the vacuum box of the altimeter. If this happens at night or in a fog, the pilot may think that he is high enough to fly over a mountain range when he really is too low to avoid crashing into the mountain.

Air-pressure altimeters are still used on small planes, but large planes use electronic altimeters. These make use of radar or radio waves which tell the pilot how high he is actually flying above any part of the earth's surface.

THERMOMETER

When you think of temperature, you probably think of feelings of heat and cold. These feelings can be misleading. In winter, people indoors may feel that a house is uncomfortably cool, but a person coming into the house from a snowstorm would feel warm. If you touch a sheet of paper which is at a temperature of 32° Fahrenheit and a sheet of aluminum at the same temperature, the aluminum will feel much colder. Since feeling is not a good guide to temperature, we need an instrument that will measure temperature without depending on the feelings of one or another individual person. A *thermometer* is such an instrument. There are a number of different kinds of thermometers. The temperature that they measure is the hotness of an object. And hotness depends on the average energy of the molecules that make up the object.

GLASS-AND-LIQUID THERMOMETER

The glass-and-liquid thermometer is the best-known device for measuring temperature. It consists of a sealed, thick-walled glass tube that contains a liquid (Fig. 53). The bottom of the tube is expanded into a thin-walled reservoir, the *bulb*. The part above the bulb is the *stem*, and the long narrow space inside the stem is the *bore*. The bulb holds the main part of the liquid. Mercury and colored alcohol are the most commonly used liquids. Both are easy to see within the glass tube. To make it even easier to see the liquid, well-made thermometers have a background strip of opaque white glass molded into the stem behind the bore. The bore is only about $\frac{1}{50}$ of an inch wide, but the outer shape of the stem is molded so that it acts as a magnifying glass. You see liquid in the bore as a line, or column, about $\frac{1}{16}$ of an inch wide. Most household thermometers have the stem mounted on a background strip of

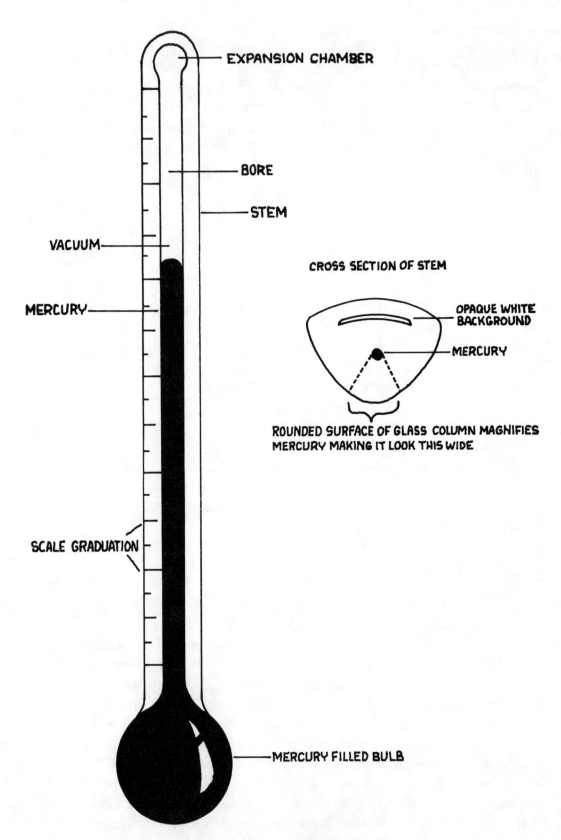

EXPANSION CHAMBER

BORE

STEM

VACUUM

MERCURY

CROSS SECTION OF STEM

OPAQUE WHITE BACKGROUND

MERCURY

ROUNDED SURFACE OF GLASS COLUMN MAGNIFIES MERCURY MAKING IT LOOK THIS WIDE

SCALE GRADUATION

MERCURY FILLED BULB

FIGURE 53

metal or wood upon which the lines of a temperature scale are printed. Thermometers used in scientific work usually have the lines of the temperature scale cut into the glass and filled with black enamel that is hardened by baking.

When the temperature surrounding the bulb increases, heat quickly passes through the wall of the bulb, raising the temperature of the liquid. The warmed liquid expands, and this causes it to rise in the bore. If the temperature surrounding the bulb decreases, heat rapidly passes out of the bulb. This cools the liquid, which contracts and moves down within the bore.

There are a number of different temperature scales. The two best known are the *Celsius*, or *centigrade*, and the *Fahrenheit* (Fig. 54). The Celsius scale is arranged so that 0° is the temperature at which water freezes, and 100° is the temperature at which water boils. The Fahrenheit scale has freezing at 32° and boiling at 212°.

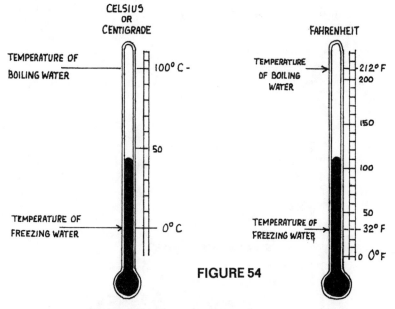

FIGURE 54

When a glass-and-liquid thermometer is being made, all the air is removed from the bore before the stem is sealed. If air were allowed to remain, the rising liquid would compress the air. The compressed air would push down on the top of the column of liquid. The higher the liquid rose, the more strongly the air would push against the liquid. A one-degree increase in temperature in the lower part of the stem would cause the liquid to rise farther than a one-degree increase near the top of the stem. This would prevent the thermometer from recording temperature accurately. When there is no air in the bore, however, the liquid rises evenly all the way to the top.

MEDICAL THERMOMETER

A special kind of glass-and-liquid thermometer is the *medical, clinical*, or *fever*, thermometer. Its scale ranges between 94° and 108° Fahrenheit. This range is wide enough, since the normal temperature of the human body is between 98° and 99°, and rarely goes below 94° or above 108°, even in the severest illnesses. A change of ⅒ of a degree in body temperature is important, so some way must be found for the liquid in the bore to remain at the highest temperature it reaches. It must not go down at all in the few seconds between the time a doctor takes the thermometer out of a patient's mouth and then reads it. The bottom of the bore has two very short, narrow lengths separated by a tiny round chamber (Fig. 55). When the bulb is warmed, the expanding mercury has enough force to push through the narrow parts of the bore. When the bulb cools, the mercury below the narrow parts contracts and pulls away from the rest of the column. The weight of the upper part of the column does not have enough force to push the mercury down through the

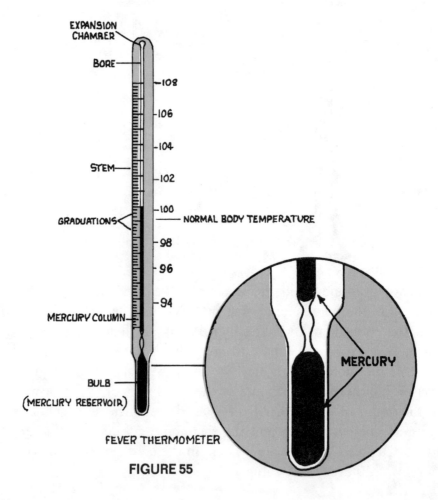

FEVER THERMOMETER

FIGURE 55

narrow parts of the bore. This leaves the top of the column at the highest mark on the scale it reached. After the doctor has read the thermometer, he moves the upper part of the mercury column down into the bulb by shaking the thermometer with a whipping motion.

METAL THERMOMETERS

Instead of an expanding and contracting liquid, some thermometers use a *bimetallic strip* (Fig. 56) . This is made up of strips of two different metals bound together tightly. One metal expands or contracts more than the other for each degree of temperature change. This causes the bimetallic strip to bend. In the thermometer, the bimetallic strip is in the shape of a nearly circular curve or a spiral. One end is fixed tightly so that it cannot move. The other end is free to move as the strip bends. The free

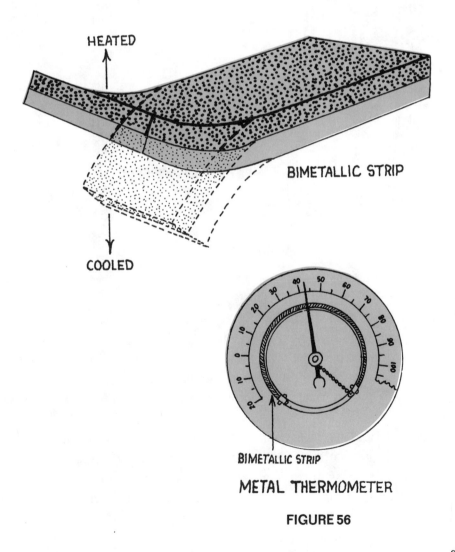

HEATED

COOLED

BIMETALLIC STRIP

BIMETALLIC STRIP

METAL THERMOMETER

FIGURE 56

end may be attached to a small chain that is wound around the axle of a pointer that moves over a temperature scale. The axle is attached to a weak spring that holds the pointer at the lowest number on the scale. When the temperature increases, the bimetallic strip curves in the direction shown by the arrow. This movement pulls on the chain, moving the pointer along the scale. When the temperature decreases, the bimetallic strip moves in the opposite direction, letting the chain become slack. The spring turns the pointer toward the opposite end of the scale. Oven thermometers use bimetallic strips, and so do thermostats (Fig. 57).

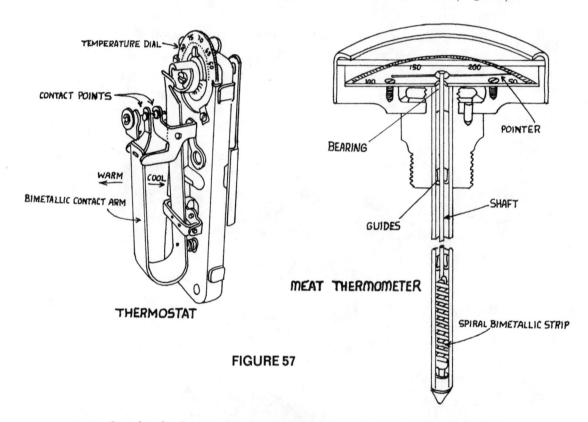

FIGURE 57

One kind of meat thermometer also uses a bimetallic strip. The strip is a long narrow coil within a hollow metal rod (Fig. 57). The upper end of the strip is attached to a solid metal rod that is held in place by guides. A pointer is attached to the upper end of this rod. As the bimetallic strip expands and contracts, the pointer moves around a temperature scale on a dial.

Scientists and engineers may want a record of temperature changes that go on in a scientific experiment or an industrial process over a long period. To obtain such a record, they use a *thermograph*, or recording thermometer (Fig. 58). This device uses a bimetallic strip, to one end of which is attached a pen with an automatic supply of ink. A wide strip

PEN

REVOLVING STRIP OF GRAPH PAPER

THERMOGRAPH, OR RECORDING THERMOMETER
FIGURE 58

of graph paper is wound around a cylinder that is turned slowly by clock-work. The cylinder may make one turn in a day or a week. During that time, as temperature changes, the bimetallic strip moves the pen across the paper, drawing a line that shows all changes in temperature.

GASOLINE DISPENSER, or GAS PUMP

When a service station attendant hears a driver say, "Fill 'er up!" he switches on the *gasoline dispenser*, which is the tall boxlike structure that most people call a "gas pump." The attendant pokes the nozzle of a hose into the opening in the car's gas tank and presses a trigger on the nozzle. This lets gasoline flow into the tank. If the nozzle has an automatic valve, the attendant can walk away from the hose to wipe the car's windshield or check the oil and water, because the nozzle will stop the flow of gasoline when the tank is filled.

The gasoline comes from an underground storage tank (Fig. 59-A). The tank has a hole at the top. A pipe, called a ventline, runs through the hole and then opens above the ground. When gasoline is pumped into the tank from tank-trucks that bring it to the filling station, air bubbles entering with gasoline escape through the ventline.

The dispenser is always filled with gasoline, right up to the nozzle. When the attendant switches on the dispenser, a pump run by an electric motor sends gasoline into a loop of the pipe. The gasoline goes around and around the loop until the attendant opens the nozzle by pulling the trigger. When the attendant does this, the pump sends gasoline into the *air eliminator tank*.

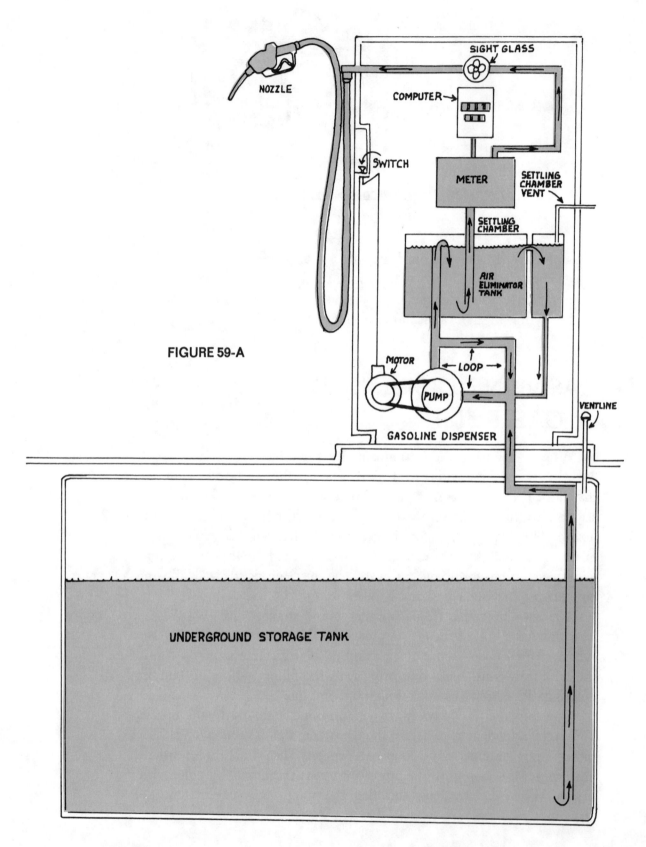

FIGURE 59-A

SIGHT GLASS

NOZZLE

COMPUTER→

SWITCH

METER

SETTLING CHAMBER VENT

SETTLING CHAMBER

AIR ELIMINATOR TANK

MOTOR

←LOOP→

PUMP

GASOLINE DISPENSER

VENTLINE

UNDERGROUND STORAGE TANK

Gasoline is pumped out of the tank through a pipe that opens near the bottom of the tank. The gasoline at the bottom is under pressure caused by the weight of the gasoline above as well as the weight of the atmosphere that enters the ventline. This pressure holds some air dissolved in the gasoline. When the gasoline has been pumped into the dispenser, the pressure is greatly lessened. As a result, the dissolved air forms bubbles in the dispenser. The air bubbles must be removed so that only gasoline goes into the car's gas tank. To get rid of the bubbles, the gasoline is pumped into the *air eliminator tank*. Here, the bubbles rise to the top of the tank and run off—with a little gasoline they carry along—into the *settling chamber*. Air from the bubbles goes out of the settling chamber through a pipe, the *settling chamber vent*, that opens to the outside of the dispenser. Pressure of the air at the top of the air eliminator tank pushes gasoline up a pipe to the *meter*. Here gasoline is measured in two *cylinders*, which are round chambers that contain *pistons* (Fig. 59-B). Some meters have only one piston; others have up to five. A rod connects each cylinder to the midsection of a *crankshaft*, which turns within *rings* on the inner ends of the rods.

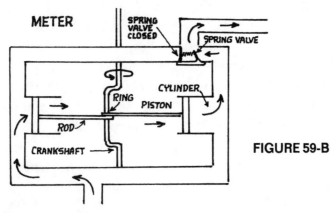

FIGURE 59-B

As gasoline flows into one cylinder (the left one in Figure 59-B) of a two-cylinder meter, the piston of that cylinder is pushed inward. This causes the piston rod to push the crankshaft around one-half turn. As the middle section moves around, it shoves the right-hand piston outward. This pushes gasoline out of the cylinder and produces enough pressure within the gasoline to force open one of two *spring valves*. Gasoline flowing through the valve goes out of the meter.

When the right-hand piston reaches the outside end of the cylinder, it no longer is pushing gasoline, so the pressure it has produced ends and the right-hand valve closes. Then the gasoline flows from the eliminator tank into the right-hand cylinder. The right-hand piston, in its turn, is pushed inward, giving the crankshaft another half turn. This shoves the left-hand piston to the end of its cylinder. Gasoline is pushed out of the left-hand cylinder and through the left-hand spring valve.

Two cylinderfuls of gasoline give the crankshaft one complete turn. Gears attached to the crankshaft turn a second set of gears. The number of teeth in the gears is arranged so that when a gear makes ten turns, the gear to its left makes one turn. Wheels are attached to the axles on which the gears turn. Numbers are printed on the rims of the wheels. On those that you see through the upper row of windows, the numbers run from 1 to 10, and there are four wheels. They show the amount of money in dollars and cents that you must pay for the gasoline pumped into the tank of your car. The lower row of windows shows how many gallons and tenths of gallons have been pumped into your car. The two rows of wheels are called the *computer*, and they are parts of an analog computer. (See Analog Computers in the section of this book on COMPUTERS.)

Most dispensers have a *sight glass* above the computer. This is a round glass lens set into a cylinder that opens into a pipe carrying gasoline from the meter to the nozzle. Within the cylinder is a small paddle wheel that is spun around by the gasoline flowing through the pipe. The sight glass lets you see that the dispenser is filled with gasoline from the start of the pumping. As the gasoline flows and the paddle wheel spins, it shows that gasoline actually is flowing into the hose.

Attached to the free end of the hose is the *automatic dispenser nozzle* (Fig. 59-C). When the attendant puts this kind of nozzle into the gas tank of a car, he pulls the trigger. If he pulls it up only partway, he can cut off the flow of gasoline simply by letting go of the trigger. But if he pulls it up higher, one end of the trigger becomes caught in a notch in the *spring clip*. This holds the trigger in the "open" position. As the

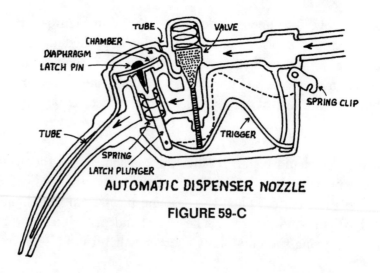

AUTOMATIC DISPENSER NOZZLE

FIGURE 59-C

trigger moves up, it pushes a *valve* up and the *latch plunger* down. These two actions open a channel for gasoline to flow out of the tip of the nozzle. As gasoline flows past the open end of a tube that leads to one end of the *diaphragm chamber*, air is drawn into the chamber through a narrow tube. This tube runs downward from the other end of the chamber almost to the outlet of the nozzle. The tube is closed at its end, but has a hole near the end. The hole opens to an equally small hole in the wall of the nozzle.

When gasoline rises high enough in the gas tank of the car to close off the hole in the nozzle, the narrow tube fills up and pushes a little gasoline into the diaphragm chamber. It compresses the air trapped there. This compressed air pushes down the rubber diaphragm and the *latch pin* attached to it. When the latch pin hits the *latch plunger*, it pushes the end of the trigger down just far enough to release the other end of the trigger from the spring clip. The released trigger springs down, freeing the valve, and another spring located above the valve pushes it shut. This stops the flow of gasoline into the gas tank.

AEROSOL CONTAINER, or SPRAY CAN

Almost every home has one or more *aerosol containers*. You probably call them "spray cans." When you push a small plastic button at the top, the container sprays a fine mist of any of a number of liquids, such as insecticides, perfumes, deodorants, air-fresheners, paints and lacquers, furniture polishes, and window and wall cleaners. The mist is an *aerosol*—droplets of liquid scattered in air. The droplets are so tiny that they can remain suspended in air for a long time.

An aerosol container is a sturdy can with a dome-shaped top and bottom, which add strength (Fig. 60). The lower half of the container holds the liquid. The upper half is filled with a gas, usually nitrogen, which is under pressure. The gas occupies the upper half because it is lighter than the liquid. Extending through the top of the container is a stiff, thin, plastic pipe, called the *plunger*. Fitting tightly over the lower end of the plunger is a flexible plastic tube, the *dip tube*, which extends down almost to the bottom of the container. Just above the place where the plunger and dip tube meet is a *valve*. It is held shut by the pressure of the gas. The upper end of the plunger fits into the bottom of the *cap*.

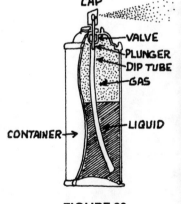

FIGURE 60

91

This is a small plastic cylinder. A round channel extends vertically from the bottom of the cap and halfway up its length. Meeting this channel at a right angle is another channel, this one very narrow.

The cap may have a shape other than the one shown in the illustration, but the purpose of all spray-can caps is to open the valve when you press the cap with your finger. Because the gas is under pressure, it is constantly pushing down on the liquid. When the valve opens, the gas forces some liquid up through the dip tube and plunger. The swiftly rising liquid strikes the top of the channel in the cap. This breaks the liquid into small droplets. The liquid being pushed up behind them forces the droplets out the narrow hole in the cap, creating a fine mist—the aerosol.

To use an aerosol can properly, you must hold it right-side-up. If you turn it upside down or tilt it too far, the bottom of the dip tube will no longer be in the liquid, but in the gas. Then, when you open the valve, a small amount of liquid that was in the dip tube will spray out. After that, only gas will come out.

The principle of the aerosol container is also used to force thick liquids, such as whipped cream, out of cans. This kind of container has no dip tube, and the plunger has a wide opening and no cap. To use it, you shake it well and turn it upside down. Shaking mixes the contents and the gas, making a foam. Because the gas is part of the more solid material, gas pressure is spread out evenly throughout the contents. Then, when the can is upside down, gas pressure pushes the foam out of the plunger.

FIRE EXTINGUISHER

There are two ways to extinguish a fire. You can lower the temperature of the burning material below its kindling point or you can prevent air from coming into contact with the burning material. Air contains oxygen which must be present if burning is to take place. Fire extinguishers do one or both of the things necessary to put out a fire.

CLASSES OF FIRE

Fire-fighting experts have divided fires into classes according to the kind of material that is burning. Each class of fire is best extinguished with a particular kind of extinguisher.

Class A fires are in wood, paper, cloth, and other ordinary burnable materials. These materials form glowing coals which are most easily extinguished by cooling them below their kindling temperatures.

Class B fires are in oil, gasoline, kerosene, paint thinners, fats, greases, and other flammable liquids. These liquids float on water and spread a fire when water is used to try to extinguish them. The best way to extinguish Class B fires is to smother them by separating them from air.

Class C fires are in electrically charged equipment and machines. Water can conduct electric current. A person playing a hose on an electrical fire may be electrocuted by current conducted through the stream of water. Therefore, only materials that do not conduct electricity should be used to extinguish Class C fires.

WATER-PUMP EXTINGUISHER

When you put water on burning material, you accomplish both things that will extinguish fire. First, when water comes into contact with the hot surface of the burning material, some water turns to steam. The heat that turns the water to steam comes from the burning material, and therefore cools it. Second, the steam forms a temporary blanket that

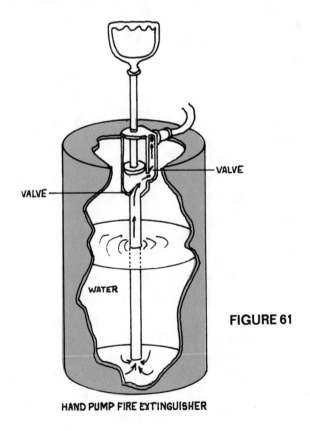

FIGURE 61

HAND PUMP FIRE EXTINGUISHER

93

separates the burning material from air. An advantage to using water to put out a fire is that water is plentiful and cheap.

In places where there are no water pipes to which to connect a hose, the water-pump fire extinguisher (Fig. 61) can be used. It consists of an enclosed tank small enough to be carried by one person. A simple lift pump directly under the top of the tank pulls water up from the bottom and forces it through a hose tipped with a nozzle. The pump is worked by a handle on top of the extinguisher. Water-pump extinguishers should be used only on Class A fires.

CARBON DIOXIDE EXTINGUISHER

Carbon dioxide is a gas that cannot support burning. It also is heavier than air. Spraying carbon dioxide upon a fire covers it with a nonburnable, heavier-than-air blanket that separates the burning material from air.

SODA-ACID EXTINGUISHER. A soda-acid extinguisher is one source of carbon dioxide. This extinguisher consists of a cylindrical copper tank, closed at both ends (Fig. 62-A). The tank is filled to the top with a solution of sodium bicarbonate (baking soda) in water. Suspended in the upper part of the tank is a glass vial within a lead cylinder. The vial is filled with sulfuric acid and is closed with a loose-fitting lead stopper. From the shoulder of the tank, a bent tube connects with a rubber hose tipped with a nozzle.

To use the extinguisher, you turn it upside down. The stopper falls out of the vial and sulfuric acid mixes with the sodium bicarbonate solution. This mixture causes a very rapid chemical reaction that forms carbon dioxide and more water as two of its products. Much of the carbon dioxide bubbles to the top of the tank (actually the bottom, since the tank is upside down) where it produces a pressure of about 75 pounds per square inch. This pushes the water and many bubbles of carbon dioxide out of the tank and sprays them upon the fire. The burning material is covered both with water that lowers the temperature and with carbon dioxide that separates it from air.

Another kind of soda-acid extinguisher (Fig. 62-B) has a completely enclosed glass vial filled with sulfuric acid at the bottom of a cone-shaped tank. Below the vial is a metal rod, or pin, with a knob at its lower end and a point at the upper end. The knob projects from the bottom of the tank, and the pointed upper end almost touches the vial. To use the extinguisher, you hit the knob sharply. The point moves upward, striking the vial and breaking it. The sulfuric acid mixes with the sodium bicarbonate solution, producing carbon dioxide.

94

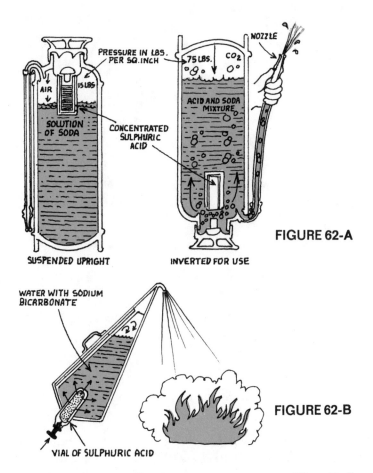

PRESSURE IN LBS.
PER SQ. INCH

AIR

15 LBS

SOLUTION
OF SODA

CONCENTRATED
SULPHURIC
ACID

SUSPENDED UPRIGHT

NOZZLE

75 LBS. CO_2

ACID AND SODA
MIXTURE

INVERTED FOR USE

FIGURE 62-A

WATER WITH SODIUM
BICARBONATE

VIAL OF SULPHURIC ACID

FIGURE 62-B

FOAM EXTINGUISHER. A very effective way to put out Class B fires is to cover them with a foam composed of bubbles of a nonburnable gas and a sticky liquid.

A foam fire extinguisher looks and works like a soda-acid extinguisher, except that it uses alum instead of sulfuric acid. Also, a material that forms a sticky liquid is mixed with the the sodium bicarbonate solution. Licorice, animal protein, or certain plastics are among the materials used. The mixture of alum and sodium bicarbonate forms carbon dioxide. The stream of bubbly liquid that squirts out of the extinguisher forms a thick, long-lasting foam upon the burning material. The light foam will float on oil, gasoline, and other flammable liquids. Foam fire extinguishers may be used on Class A and B fires, but not on Class C.

LIQUID CARBON DIOXIDE EXTINGUISHER. Another kind of carbon dioxide extinguisher consists of a strong metal cylinder two-thirds full of liquid carbon dioxide (Fig. 63). The carbon dioxide is in liquid form because it is under pressure of more than 1,000 pounds per square inch. The pressure comes from the gaseous carbon dioxide that fills the upper third of the tank. At the top of the tank there is a valve with a handle for opening it. A tube leads up from near the bottom of the tank to the

95

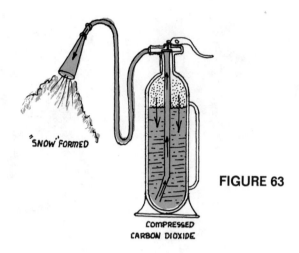

"SNOW" FORMED

FIGURE 63

COMPRESSED
CARBON DIOXIDE

valve. Leading outward from the valve is a hose that ends in a long, wide-mouthed plastic nozzle.

To use the extinguisher, you open the valve by pressing on the handle. The gas within the tank pushes liquid carbon dioxide up the tube and through the hose to the nozzle. In the nozzle, more than two-thirds of the liquid immediately becomes a gas, expanding as it does. The expansion causes the liquid to lose heat so rapidly that it freezes the other one-third to carbon dioxide snow. The snow is sprayed on the fire. It instantly changes to a gas. This cools the burning material and covers it with a nonburnable blanket of carbon dioxide gas. A carbon dioxide fire extinguisher may be used on Class A, B, and C fires.

DRY-CHEMICAL EXTINGUISHER. A dry-chemical extinguisher (Fig. 64) consists of a tank containing powdered sodium bicarbonate. Also, inside the tank is a smaller tank filled with carbon dioxide or nitrogen gas under pressure. To use the extinguisher, you turn a control knob that lets gas out of the small tank. This pushes powdered sodium bicarbonate out of the wide-mouthed spout of the larger tank. When particles of the sodium bicarbonate powder fall upon the burning material, they are heated. At a temperature of 518° Fahrenheit (270° Celsius), they give off carbon dioxide gas. Dry-chemical extinguishers may be used on Class B and C fires.

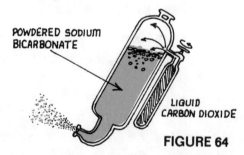

POWDERED SODIUM
BICARBONATE

LIQUID
CARBON DIOXIDE

FIGURE 64

CARBON TETRACHLORIDE EXTINGUISHER

Carbon tetrachloride is a liquid that does not burn. It changes to gas at 169.8° F. (76.5° C.), forming a heavier-than-air nonburnable gas that can smother fires. One kind of carbon tetrachloride extinguisher (Fig. 65-A) is a small cylindrical tank that can be held in one hand. Inside the top of the tank is a pump and the pump handle extends through the top of the tank. A nozzle opens from the front. To use the extinguisher, you give the handle a part-turn so as to free it. Then you simply pump carbon tetrachloride on the fire.

FIGURE 65-A

A second type of carbon tetrachloride extinguisher uses pressure produced by vaporizing liquid carbon tetrachloride (Fig. 65-B).

You probably have seen ruby glass globes hanging from the ceilings of public buildings. These are filled with carbon tetrachloride. The fixture from which the globes hang (Fig. 65-C) is made of a metal alloy that

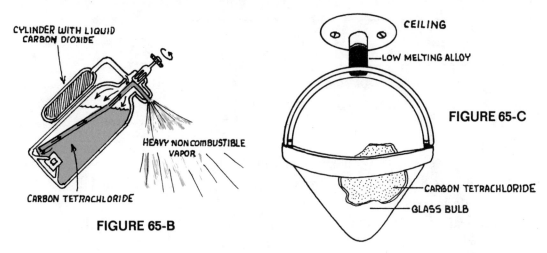

FIGURE 65-B

FIGURE 65-C

melts at a temperature of about 200° F. (93.3° C.). Heat from a fire melts the alloy. The globes fall to the floor and shatter, splashing carbon tetrachloride on the fire.

Carbon tetrachloride fire extinguishers may be used on Class B and C fires.

PHOTOELECTRIC CELL, or ELECTRIC EYE

Perhaps you've walked up to the entrance of a large building or store and when you were close enough to push on the door, it opened by itself.

Then, when you had passed through the door, it closed. Neither you nor anyone else had touched the door. It was opened and closed by machinery controlled by a photocell, or "electric eye."

When light shines upon certain metals, they give off electrons. Metals that do this are said to be *photoelectric*. Among them are the chemical elements cesium, lithium, potassium, and sodium. These metals are used to make *photoelectric cells*, or simply, *photocells*.

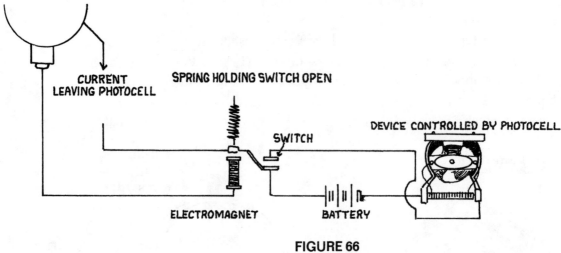

FIGURE 66

There are several kinds of photocells. One (Fig. 66) consists of a glass bulb that has the inside coated with a photoelectric metal. The outside is coated with a material through which light cannot pass. A small, clear, circular window is left in both coatings. A glass lens in front of the window concentrates the incoming light upon the photoelectric coating at the opposite side of the bulb. In the center of the bulb, just below the window, is a metal knob (or a plate) called the *anode*. It is charged electrically positive by being connected to the positive pole of a battery or other electric device.

Electrons are unit charges of negative electricity. When light enters the window of a photocell, the photoelectric coating gives off great numbers of electrons. These stream to the anode. They do so in accord with the Law of Electric Charges which says, in part, that positive and negative charges attract each other. The stream of electrons makes up an electric current. This current is weak, so it must be strengthened by sending it through a transistorized circuit or some other kind of a current magnifier.

The photocell which is part of machinery that opens a door is built into the wall at one side of the doorway (Fig. 67). A light projector is

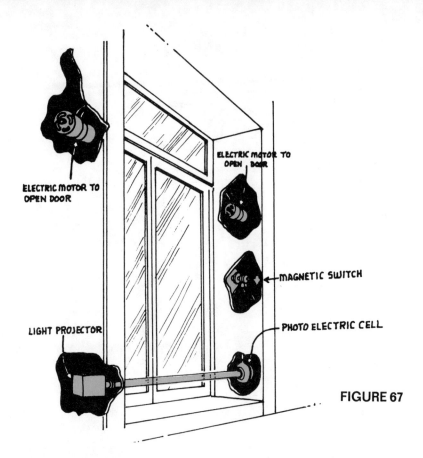

ELECTRIC MOTOR TO
OPEN DOOR

ELECTRIC MOTOR TO
OPEN DOOR

MAGNETIC SWITCH

LIGHT PROJECTOR

PHOTO ELECTRIC CELL

FIGURE 67

built into the wall on the other side. The beam of light from the projector enters the photocell and causes an electric current to flow. The current goes to an electromagnet that is part of an electric switch. As long as current from the photocell is flowing, the magnet holds the switch open. When a person approaching the door walks through the light beam, light is cut off from the photocell. During this moment, no current flows from the photocell and the electromagnet ceases to work. The switch closes and electric motors connected to the door open it. The electricity to run the motors comes from a more powerful source than the photocell.

After the person has passed through the beam, current again flows from the photocell to the switch. Devices in the electric circuit delay the opening of the switch a bit, and the motors close the door.

The photocell acted as if it saw a person approach the door. For this reason, a photocell is sometimes called an *electric eye*.

Photocells have many other uses. Mounted at the front of a camera, a photocell measures the amount of light striking the lens. Current from the photocell automatically widens or narrows a diaphragm, the device that lets varying amounts of light into a camera, and thus provides proper film exposure. Photocells automatically inspect products moving on assembly belts in factories. For example, in a canning factory, each can moving through a beam of light (Fig. 68) cuts off light from the photocell for the same length of time. But a dented can will allow more light to

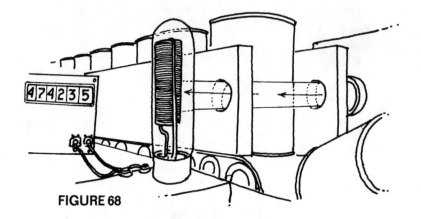

FIGURE 68

enter the photocell. The extra amount of current that flows from the photocell causes the metal arm to push that can off the assembly line.

FIREWORKS

A skyrocket streaks upward into the blackness of the night sky. It bursts, throwing outward trails of silvery fire that end in red, green, yellow, and blue stars. Then, a few seconds later, when the stars have burned out, three bombs explode thunderously in flashes of blinding white fire. A skyrocket is a spectacular favorite among several kinds of fireworks.

Fireworks are devices in which burning chemicals produce colored fire or smoke, usually accompanied by the loud noises of explosions. To propel fireworks, black gunpowder is used. The ingredients of the gunpowder are slightly changed so that the kind used in fireworks has more charcoal than ordinary black gunpowder. Charcoal causes the powder to burn more slowly. This powder is called simply *black powder*.

The colored lights called *stars* are made from a number of different substances, depending on the color wanted. The color-producing chemical is mixed with a slow-burning material such as sawdust, and the mixture is held together with a gummy material, such as gum arabic.

SKYROCKET

A skyrocket consists of two hollow cylinders (Fig. 69). In the rear cylinder is a *booster*, or *propelling, charge* of black powder. The front cylinder contains a *bursting* charge of black powder, within which are stars and noise bombs, and possibly a parachute. The top of this cylinder is closed by a clay cap. The two cylinders are separated by a clay plug that has holes in it. The rear end of the rear cylinder is blocked by a clay ring called a *choke*. A *fuse* runs through the choke and into the booster charge. A stick is attached to the side of the rear cylinder. The stick keeps the rocket from tumbling end over end when it is in flight.

When you light the fuse, it sets the booster charge afire. Hot gases from the burning black powder rush out the rear of the cylinder. In reaction to their motion, the rocket is boosted into the air. The booster charge burns from the rear end forward. When the burning powder reaches the front of the rear cylinder, the fire passes through the clay plug and sets the bursting charge afire. The cap is blown off and the sides of the front cylinder are blown open. The stars and bombs are hurled outward in a shower of fire. The parachute opens and keeps the bombs from falling rapidly. Fuses burn into the bombs' bursting charges which explode as the final display of the rocket.

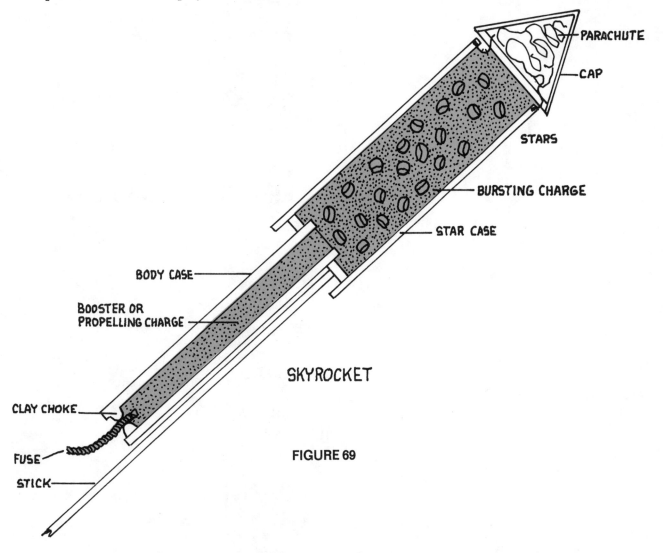

SKYROCKET

FIGURE 69

ROMAN CANDLE

A Roman candle is a narrow cardboard tube (Fig. 70) that shoots out about ten colored stars at intervals of one or two seconds. The bottom of the tube is plugged with clay and is attached to a stick which you

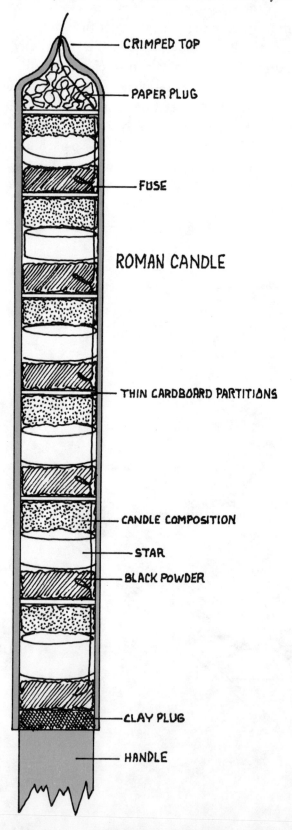

CRIMPED TOP

PAPER PLUG

FUSE

ROMAN CANDLE

THIN CARDBOARD PARTITIONS

CANDLE COMPOSITION

STAR

BLACK POWDER

CLAY PLUG

HANDLE

FIGURE 70

can hold in your hand. Directly above the clay is a small amount of black powder. Above the powder is a star, and above the star is a small amount of a slow-burning material called *candle composition*. Burning candle composition produces a streak of fire as it shoots through the air. These three things, in this order—black powder, star, candle composition—are packed into the tube over and over again, until the top of the tube is reached. A fuse runs from the top to the bottom of the tube and branches into each of the black powder charges. When you light the fuse, it sets afire the charge nearest the top of the tube. The expanding gas produced by the burning black powder shoots the star and candle composition out of the top of the tube. The fuse passes fire down the tube from charge to charge. When the second charge is set afire, it follows the first one out of the tube. This series of events continues until all the charges have shot out of the tube, making streaks of fire within which are bright stars.

PINWHEEL

A pinwheel is made up of several long paper tubes wound around a cardboard disc (Fig. 71). A pin through the center of the disc allows it to spin. The tubes contain black powder, mixed with color-producing chemicals, and steel filings or powdered iron oxide. The last two of these ingredients produce bright sparks when they burn. As the packed paper tubes burn and burning gases rush out the ends of the tubes, they cause the disc to spin rapidly and shoot out swarms of colored sparks.

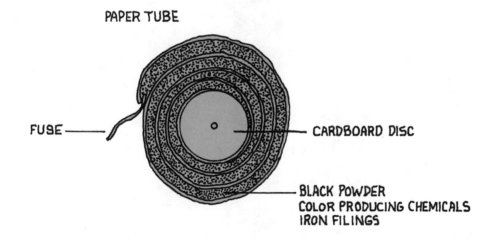

PAPER TUBE

FUSE

CARDBOARD DISC

BLACK POWDER
COLOR PRODUCING CHEMICALS
IRON FILINGS

PINWHEEL

FIGURE 71

FIRECRACKER

A firecracker is made by winding several layers of strong paper into the shape of a hollow cylinder (Fig. 72). The cylinder is filled with a powder made up of potassium chlorate, sulfur, and aluminum. The cylinder is closed at both ends by crimping the paper inward and downward. A fuse passes through one end, which then becomes the top of the firecracker. The fuse is a very narrow paper tube filled with black powder. When the free end of a fuse is set afire, it burns rapidly, carrying fire to the powder within the cylinder. The fire causes a chemical reaction that almost instantly changes the powder into gas, which has a volume many times that of the cylinder. This reaction is an explosion. It bursts the cylinder and sends outward a powerful sound wave that is the loud noise made by the firecracker.

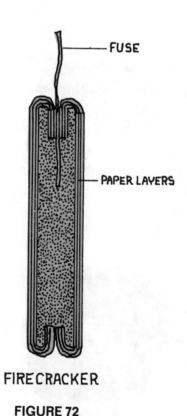

FUSE

PAPER LAYERS

FIRECRACKER

FIGURE 72

AIRCRAFT

Men have invented a number of vehicles in which they can fly. These include airplanes, gliders, balloons, dirigibles, helicopters, and air-cushion vehicles. All of them are called aircraft.

AIRPLANE

There are more airplanes than any other kind of aircraft. The total number in the world is in the hundreds of thousands. To understand how an airplane works, we first must know how one is constructed.

FUSELAGE

The body of an airplane is the *fuselage* (Fig. 73). It is the part of the plane that carries the flight crew, passengers, and cargo. At the front end of the fuselage is the *nose*. Within the nose is a space in which the flight crew sits and which contains the controls and a panel of flight-control and navigation instruments. This space is the *cockpit*. The main part of the fuselage, where the passengers ride, is the *cabin*. The rear end is the *tail section*.

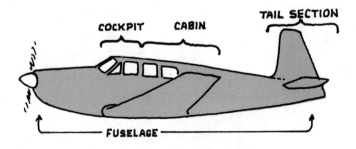

FIGURE 73

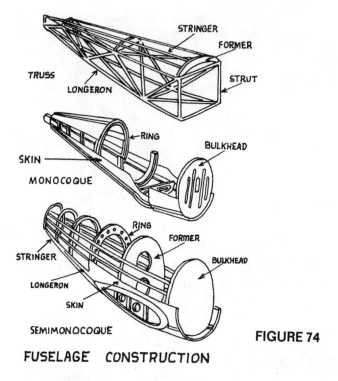

FIGURE 74

FUSELAGE CONSTRUCTION

A fuselage is a wide tube that tapers toward the rear. There are three main types of fuselages (Fig. 74). One type, the *truss* fuselage, is made up of a framework of *longerons*, which run lengthwise, and *struts*, which run crosswise and up and down. The struts and longerons are braced and strengthened by *stringers*. The framework gives the fuselage strength needed to withstand the strains experienced by an airplane in flight. Added shape is given to the fuselage by *formers*. The truss fuselage may be constructed of wooden strips or of hollow rods made of aluminum or magnesium alloys (mixtures of aluminum or magnesium with other metals). These rods are very light. The truss framework is covered by thin sheets of aluminum or magnesium alloys, plastic, fiberglass, or fabric. If fabric is used, it is coated with "dope," a liquid that shrinks the fabric, making it fit the fuselage tightly.

The *stressed-skin* fuselage consists of an outer shell strong enough to bear most of the powerful pushes and pulls that act upon an airplane in flight. Such a fuselage is strengthened with *bulkheads* which extend across the inside of the shell, and *rings* which extend around it. Stressed-skin fuselages are constructed of light-metal alloys, plastic, or fiberglass. This type of fuselage is also known as a *monocoque*, which is French for "single shell."

The most common kind of fuselage is the *semimonocoque*, a combination of the truss and stressed-shell construction. It is a stressed shell reinforced by longerons for added strength.

106

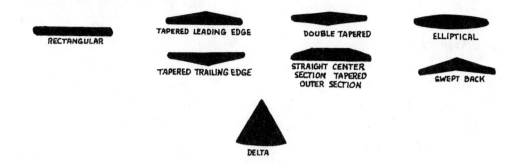

RECTANGULAR

TAPERED LEADING EDGE

DOUBLE TAPERED

ELLIPTICAL

TAPERED TRAILING EDGE

STRAIGHT CENTER SECTION TAPERED OUTER SECTION

SWEPT BACK

DELTA

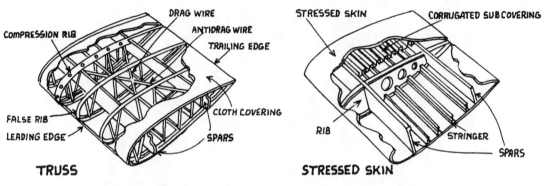

DRAG WIRE

COMPRESSION RIB

ANTIDRAG WIRE

TRAILING EDGE

STRESSED SKIN

CORRUGATED SUB COVERING

FALSE RIB

LEADING EDGE

CLOTH COVERING

SPARS

RIB

STRINGER

SPARS

TRUSS

STRESSED SKIN

CROSS SECTION AND CONSTRUCTION OF WING

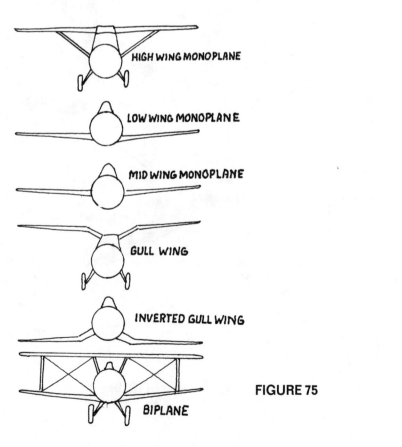

HIGH WING MONOPLANE

LOW WING MONOPLANE

MID WING MONOPLANE

GULL WING

INVERTED GULL WING

BIPLANE

FIGURE 75

107

WINGS

Airplane wings seen from above or in front have many different shapes (Fig. 75). The particular shape depends upon the purpose for which the airplane was designed. A combat plane, which must maneuver quickly, has thin wings. A cargo plane, which must carry heavy loads, has wide wings.

All airplane wings have similar shapes when seen in cross section (as if cut from front to back with a knife), because it is this shape that makes it possible for an airplane to fly.

All modern planes have one set of two wings—one wing on each side of the fuselage. These planes are *monoplanes*. A few old-fashioned planes have two sets of wings. These are *biplanes*. There are a number of ways in which wings are attached to the fuselage (Fig. 75).

The end of a wing that joins the fuselage is the *root* (Fig. 76); the other end is the *tip*. The front of a wing is the *leading edge*, and the rear is the *trailing edge*. An airplane wing is also called an *airfoil*.

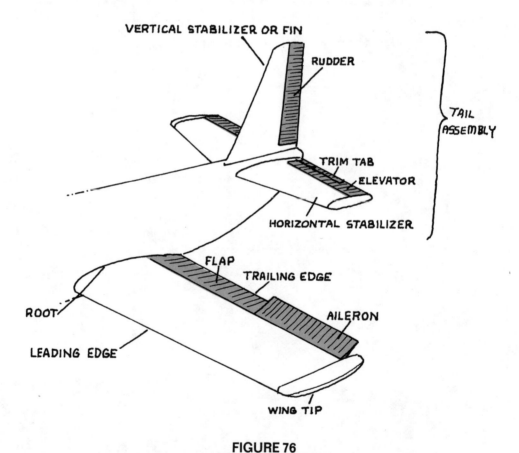

FIGURE 76

FLAPS AND AILERONS

Extending outward from the wing root on the trailing edge, about two-thirds the length of each wing, is a flat beam that is hinged to the wing (Fig. 76). This beam is a *flap*. It helps the wings lift the plane into the air and to give extra lift when the plane is landing. The pilot can raise and lower the flap on each wing by means of controls in the cockpit.

Next to the flap and extending outward to the wing tip is another hinged section called an *aileron*. It can swing both above and below the wing. Each of the two ailerons is attached (by strong wires running through pulleys within the fuselage) to a short metal pole that slants upward from the floor of the cockpit, the *control stick* (Fig. 77). In many planes, at the top of the control stick, is a structure resembling two-thirds of the steering wheel of an automobile. This is the *yoke*. The control stick can move forward and backward and to either side. The yoke moves forward and back, and turns from side to side. When a pilot turns the yoke to the right, the aileron on the right wing moves up and the aileron on the left wing moves down. When the yoke is turned to the left, the positions of the ailerons are reversed. Tipping the control stick to the right or left has the same effect. In airliners, the large size of the ailerons and the pressure of the air streaming past the wings make it too hard for the pilot to move the ailerons by his own strength. When he turns the yoke, powerful electric motors move the ailerons.

TAIL

The tail is, of course, at the rear of the fuselage. An upright surface and two horizontal surfaces make up the *tail assembly* (Fig. 76). The upright part is hinged along the middle and the rear half can swing either to the right or left. The front half is the *vertical stabilizer*, or *fin*. It keeps the tail from making unwanted movements to the right or left. The rear half is the *rudder*. It steers the plane to the right or left. In small planes, one set of wires is attached to the right side of the rudder and one set to the left side. The wires run through the fuselage to two *rudder bars* or two *rudder pedals* which are on the floor of the cockpit in front of the pilot (Fig. 77). When the pilot pushes one of the rudder pedals with his foot, he pulls on one of the wires and the rudder moves in the direction of the pull. As with ailerons, the rudder of an airliner requires much force to move, and is moved by electric motors that work on signal from the pilot as he steps on the pedals.

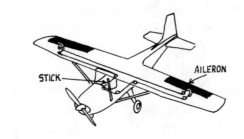

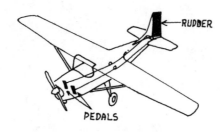

FIGURE 77

The horizontal surfaces of the tail, too, are split and hinged. The front halves are immovable. They are the *horizontal stabilizers*, which keep the tail from making unwanted up or down movements. The movable parts are *elevators*. The right and left elevators move up and down together. They are attached by wires and pulleys to the control stick in the cockpit (Fig. 77). When the pilot pushes the control stick (or yoke) forward, the elevators swing downward, and when the stick is pulled back, the elevators move up.

Many planes do not have separate horizontal stabilizers and elevators. Instead, there is a single movable surface, called a *stabilator*, on each side of the tail.

LANDING GEAR

Most airplanes take off and land on wheels. The wheels and the structure of struts and braces to which the wheels are attached make up the *undercarriage*, or *landing gear*. Small planes have two large wheels attached by struts to the fuselage beneath the wings. The wheels extend sideward beneath the fuselage and are called *outrigger wheels* (Fig. 78-A). A third wheel, the tail wheel, is located under the tail or extends downward on a strut under the nose. The arrangement that has the wheel under the tail is called *conventional* landing gear. The arrangement with the nose wheel is *tricycle* landing gear. Most large planes have tricycle landing gear with four or eight wheels in groups of two or four located beneath the wings. Another group of wheels is on a strut extending down from the nose.

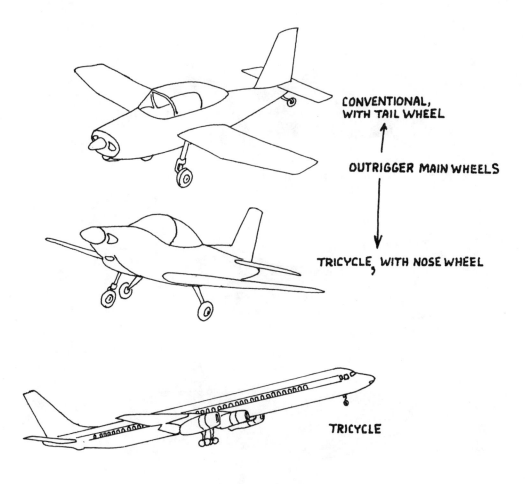

CONVENTIONAL, WITH TAIL WHEEL

OUTRIGGER MAIN WHEELS

TRICYCLE, WITH NOSE WHEEL

TRICYCLE

FIGURE 78-A

111

Some airplanes land on ice and have skis, or ice-runners, in the place of wheels. Planes that land on water substitute pontoons for wheels. Some planes can take off and land on either ground or water. These planes, called *amphibians*, have wheels that protrude downward from pontoons. Some airplanes that land on water do not have any landing gear. Their fuselage is shaped like the hull of a boat, and these planes are called *flying boats* (Fig. 78-B).

Landing gear produces a fairly large amount of resistance to the air through which an airplane flies. To do away with this resistance, medium- and large-sized airplanes have landing gear that can be folded into spaces,

ICE RUNNERS OR SKIS

AMPHIBIAN

LANDING WHEELS FOLDED INTO
WELLS ON SIDE OF FUSELAGE

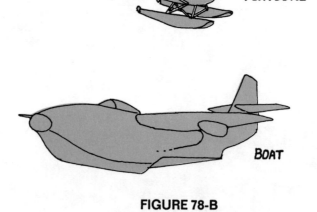

PONTOONS

BOAT

FIGURE 78-B

called *wells*, within the wings (Fig. 79). At takeoff, once a plane is safely off the ground, the pilot throws a switch and machinery folds the landing gear into the wing wells. When the airplane is approaching an airport for a landing, the machinery lowers the wheels into landing position.

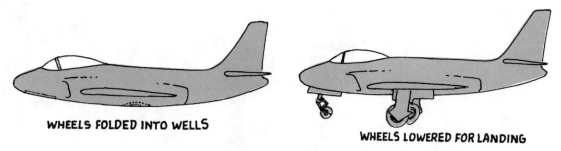

WHEELS FOLDED INTO WELLS

WHEELS LOWERED FOR LANDING

FIGURE 79

ENGINES

GASOLINE PISTON ENGINE. Small airplanes have a single engine which is at the forefront of the fuselage. Larger planes have two, three, four, six, or eight engines which may be attached to the fuselage or the wings in several different locations (Fig. 80). All small planes and many medium-sized planes have gasoline-powered internal-combustion engines that drive propellers. An internal-combustion engine burns fuel within the engine. The fuel is gasoline. Automobiles have internal-combustion engines in which the cylinders (the spaces in which gasoline is burned) are in side-by-side rows (Fig. 81). Many small plane engines have a similar cylinder arrangement. Other gasoline-powered airplane engines have cylinders arranged in a circle and are called *radial* engines. Both kinds of engines are *piston* engines. The piston is the solid cylinder that moves within the cylinder space and carries off the energy of the burning gasoline.

Gasoline in an internal-combustion engine needs the oxygen of the air in order to burn. At high altitudes there is less air per cubic foot of space than at low altitudes. Also, at high altitudes the pressure of the air is less. The lessened pressure cannot push air into the cylinders very well. A result of these two conditions of the upper atmosphere is that high-flying, gasoline-burning airplanes lack enough oxygen to burn fuel efficiently. To overcome this difficulty, the engine has a high-speed pump that pulls air through a wide tube into the engine. This device, called a *supercharger*, sends into the cylinders as much air as they would receive at low altitudes.

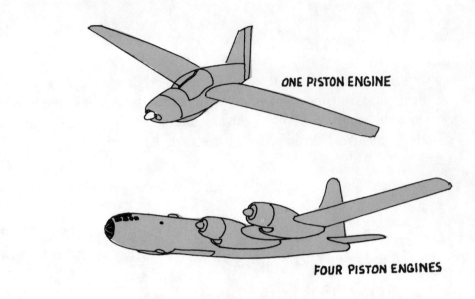

ONE PISTON ENGINE

FOUR PISTON ENGINES

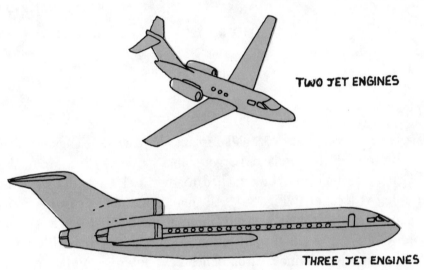

TWO JET ENGINES

THREE JET ENGINES

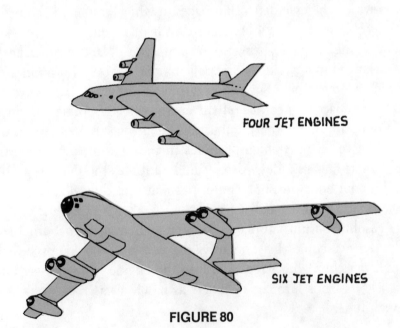

FOUR JET ENGINES

SIX JET ENGINES

FIGURE 80

114

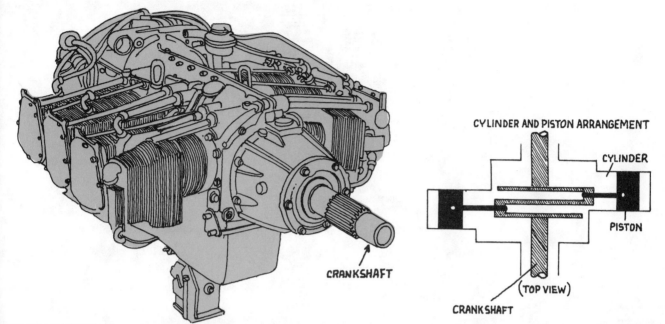

CYLINDER AND PISTON ARRANGEMENT

CYLINDER

PISTON

(TOP VIEW)

CRANK SHAFT

CRANKSHAFT

SIX CYLINDER HORIZONTALLY OPPOSED OR SIDE BY SIDE ENGINE

SIX CYLINDER HORIZONTALLY OPPOSED OR SIDE-BY-SIDE ENGINE

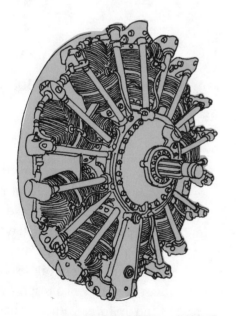

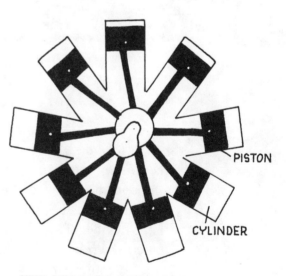

PISTON

CYLINDER

NINE CYLINDER RADIAL ENGINE

NINE CYLINDER RADIAL ENGINE

FIGURE 81

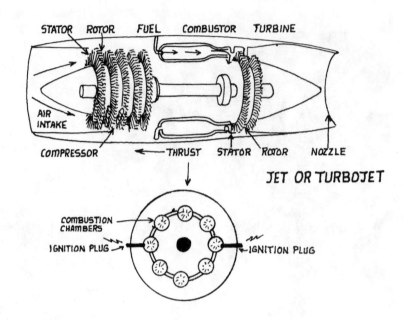

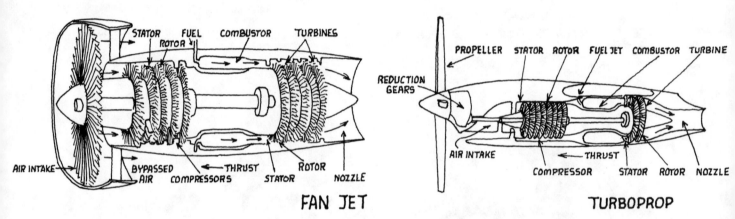

FIGURE 82

JET ENGINE. A jet engine is housed within a wide tube, called a *cowling* or *housing*, which is open at both ends (Fig. 82). Running through the center of the cowling is a strong metal shaft. Attached to the shaft near the front end of the engine are several wheels that have a large number of small blades. These make up the *compressor*. The air that enters the front end of the cowling is pushed rearward at very high speed by the compressor blades which spin at about 11,000 revolutions per minute. The air is squeezed, or compressed, and is forced into eight to twelve *combustion chambers*, thick-walled tubes arranged in a circle behind the compressor. Jet fuel (which is much like kerosene) is pumped into the combustion chambers and is burned there. The burning fuel heats the air and causes it to expand. The burning fuel turns to gas and

116

adds its volume to the expanding air. These processes greatly increase the pressure of the gases (air is a mixture of gases) in the combustion chambers. The hot gases push out of the chambers at very high speed and pass through large metal blades of a wheel called a *turbine*. The turbine is attached to the rear end of the central shaft. The gases pushing through the turbine spin the shaft, and the shaft spins the compressor wheels at the front of the cowling. The gases, having passed through the turbine, jet out of the rear of the cowling.

The most efficient and widely used type of jet engine is the *turbofan*. It is similar to the turboprop, except that the turbine, instead of turning a propeller, spins a large fan located just inside the front end of the cowling. The air is pushed rearward through the inside of the cowling. Gases that result from the burning fuel join the air from the fan. The result is a very large volume of high-speed air rushing out the rear of the cowling.

In another kind of jet engine, the front end of the shaft holds a gear which turns another shaft to which a propeller is attached. This engine is a *turboprop*. It combines the action of both a jet engine and a propeller.

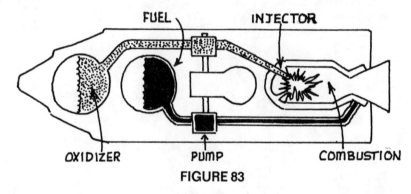

FIGURE 83

ROCKET ENGINE. Airplanes that are powered by *rocket* engines are flown in the upper stratosphere and in the near limits of outer space. Rocket-driven planes are still being flown for experimental reasons—to gain engineering information about how they work. However, very near the end of World War II, the Nazi air force flew rocket-powered fighter planes in combat.

A rocket airplane engine (Fig. 83) consists of fuel tanks and one or more combustion chambers with special exhaust nozzles. All of these are housed in a straight tube open at only one end. The engine is located in the rear two-thirds of the fuselage. The fuel may be gasoline, alcohol, kerosene, or ammonia. Oxygen is needed to burn the fuel and most commonly is provided by liquid oxygen. The fuel is stored in one tank and the liquid oxygen (which is known as the oxidizer) is in another tank. Pumps pull the liquids from the tanks and send them to the combustion chamber where burning takes place. The pumps are driven by a small turbine that is powered by a separate supply of fuel. The gases formed by the burning fuel rush out the rear of the rocket, passing through a nozzle specially shaped to give them the greatest possible speed.

FUEL. An airplane pilot controls the amount of fuel that goes to an engine by means of a *throttle*. This device is somewhat like the accelerator in an automobile. One difference is that a driver operates an accelerator by pressing on a pedal with his foot, but a pilot operates a throttle (which has a handle on the instrument panel) with his hand. Another difference is that a driver must push down constantly on the accelerator pedal in order to keep the automobile moving. If the driver removes his foot, a spring pushes the accelerator pedal up and another spring cuts off the flow of fuel to the engine. A pilot moves the throttle handle in its slot. When he removes his hand, the handle remains in the position to which he moved it, and the fuel pump continues to send fuel to the engine.

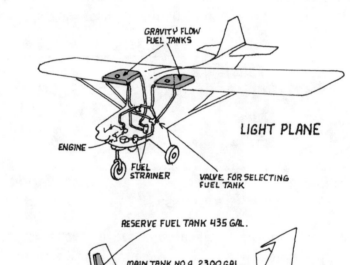

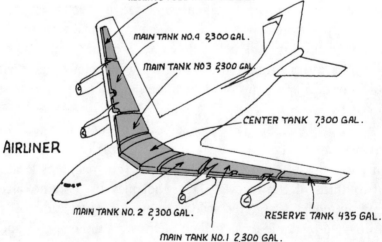

FIGURE 84

When a pilot sends more fuel to the engine, he "opens" the throttle. When he cuts down on the fuel flow, he "closes" the throttle. What he is actually doing is opening and closing a valve that regulates the flow of fuel.

Small airplanes carry gasoline in tanks that are in the wings, directly over the fuselage (Fig. 84). The force of gravity pulls the fuel down through pipes to the engine. A large airliner may carry 30,000 gallons of fuel in seven tanks which take up almost all the space within the wings. By putting fuel tanks into the wings instead of in the fuselage, cabin space is made available in the fuselage. Pumps send fuel from the tanks to the engines.

PROPELLERS

A propeller blade is an airfoil having a leading edge and a trailing edge (Fig. 85). Blades may be made of wood, aluminum, or steel. One end of each blade is affixed into sockets at the end of a metal shaft which is turned by the engine. Blades on opposite sides of the shaft face in opposite directions. Propellers that drive small planes usually have only two blades. Propellers on large planes may have two to six blades.

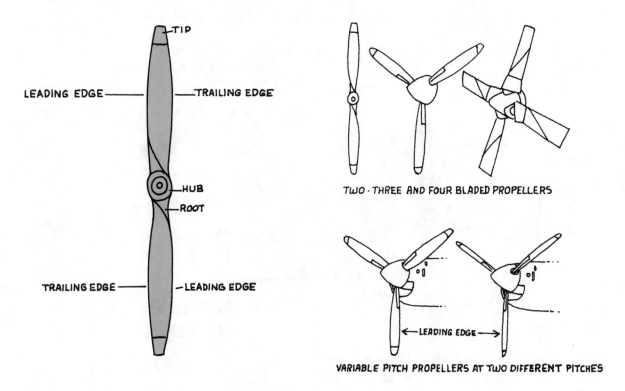

FIGURE 85

Propellers work best if they deliver different amounts of force at different times during a flight. The blades must spin the fastest and throw the most air when an airplane is climbing, as when it is taking off from an airport. Once the plane is in the air, the propellers work better if they scoop less air. To vary the working performance of a propeller, there is an arrangement of gears within the sockets to which the blades are affixed. The gears turn the blades around a line through the center of their lengths. The pilot can control the gears from the cockpit. Turning a blade changes the angle between its leading edge and the direction in which the propeller is turning. This angle is the *pitch* of the blade. Propellers in which the pitch of the blades can be changed are *variable-pitch*, or *controllable-pitch*, propellers. Different flying speeds and maneuvers require different propeller pitches. *Constant-speed* propellers automatically change pitch, keeping the plane's engine speed unchanged.

INSTRUMENTS

In order to keep his airplane flying well and to navigate it to his destination, a pilot must know many things about the condition of the plane and what is happening outside it. A plane has a number of *instruments* that measure flying conditions and indicate them on dials and gauges which are on the *instrument panel* in front of the pilot (Fig. 86).

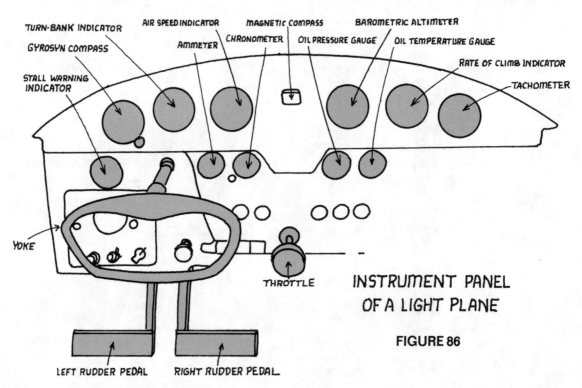

INSTRUMENT PANEL
OF A LIGHT PLANE

FIGURE 86

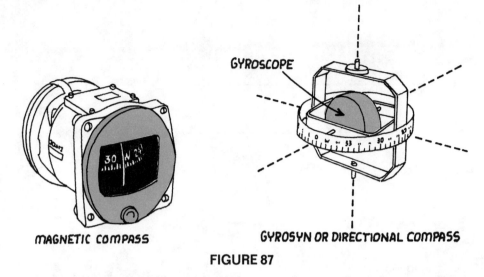

GYROSCOPE

MAGNETIC COMPASS

GYROSYN OR DIRECTIONAL COMPASS

FIGURE 87

A *magnetic compass* (Fig. 87) tells the pilot in which direction the plane is flying. This compass works well during steady, level flight. When an airplane makes sudden, fast turns, rolls, or dives, a magnetic compass swings widely off the mark and is temporarily useless to the pilot. Because of this, the instrument panel includes a *gyrosyn*, or *directional*, *compass*. This compass contains a gyroscope which keeps the compass pointing north, as a magnetic compass does, but remains on the mark when the plane suddenly changes direction.

The *air-speed indicator* (Fig. 88-A) tells a pilot how fast the plane is moving through the air, which is a speed different from how fast the plane is moving over the earth's surface (Fig. 88-B).

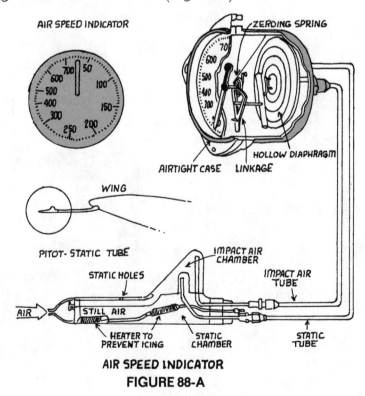

AIR SPEED INDICATOR

ZEROING SPRING

HOLLOW DIAPHRAGM

AIRTIGHT CASE   LINKAGE

WING

PITOT-STATIC TUBE

STATIC HOLES

IMPACT AIR CHAMBER

IMPACT AIR TUBE

AIR

STILL AIR

HEATER TO PREVENT ICING

STATIC CHAMBER

STATIC TUBE

AIR SPEED INDICATOR
FIGURE 88-A

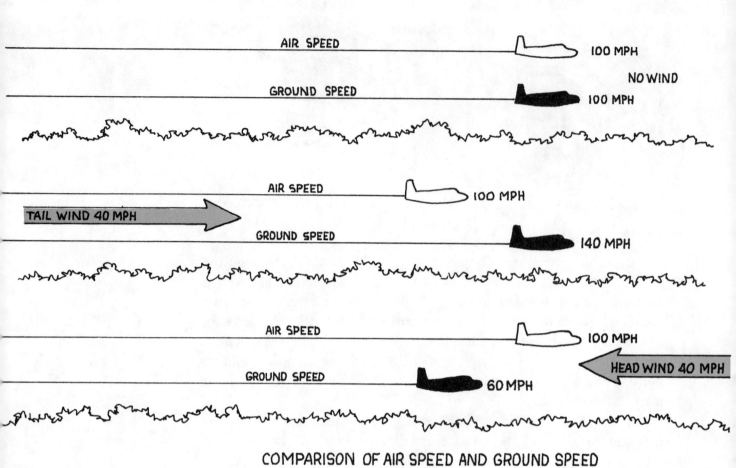

AIR SPEED   100 MPH

                                             NO WIND
GROUND SPEED   100 MPH

AIR SPEED   100 MPH

TAIL WIND 40 MPH

GROUND SPEED   140 MPH

AIR SPEED   100 MPH

                                    HEAD WIND 40 MPH

GROUND SPEED   60 MPH

COMPARISON OF AIR SPEED AND GROUND SPEED
FIGURE 88-B

The *horizon indicator* (Fig. 89) shows an artificial horizon that corresponds to the real horizon. This instrument is very important at night and in stormy weather when the pilot cannot see the real horizon.

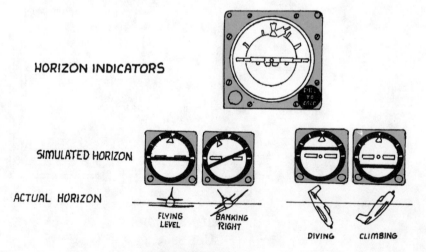

HORIZON INDICATORS

SIMULATED HORIZON

ACTUAL HORIZON

FLYING LEVEL   BANKING RIGHT   DIVING   CLIMBING

FIGURE 89

The *turn-and-bank indicator* (Fig. 90) shows the pilot the angle at which his plane is tipped when he is turning, and whether his plane is skidding or slipping.

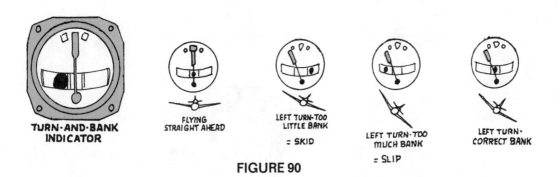

FIGURE 90

The pilot finds his altitude by looking at the *altimeter*. There are altimeters that work by means of the pressure of the atmosphere and altimeters that work by radio or radar (Fig. 91).

ALTIMETERS

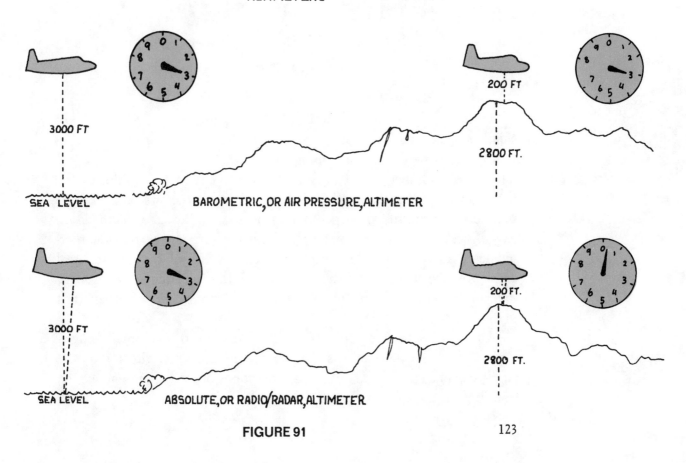

FIGURE 91

123

A *two-way radio*—one that both receives and broadcasts messages—keeps the pilot in touch with ground stations, especially airports from which he must get his takeoff and landing instructions. He also receives constant weather reports on the radio. And he may navigate to his destination by following a beam of radio signals.

A *chronometer*, a very accurate clock, not only tells time, but helps the pilot to make the calculations he needs for navigating.

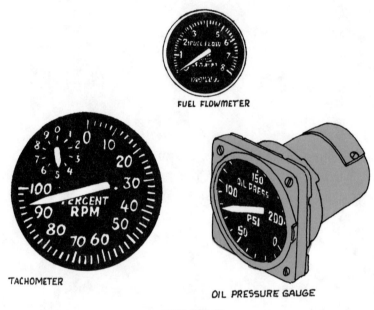

FUEL FLOWMETER

TACHOMETER

OIL PRESSURE GAUGE

FIGURE 92

If the engine of an airplane is not working properly, the pilot cannot simply stop and walk to a phone to call a service station for help. He constantly needs to know many things about the condition of his engine. There are a number of instruments that continually tell the pilot of the performance of the engine (Fig. 92). A *tachometer* shows on a dial the number of turns the propeller is making each minute. A *temperature gauge*, which is part of a metal thermometer (see the section on thermometers in this book), indicates the temperature of the engine. And an *oil-pressure gauge* shows the pressure of oil in the engine. *Fuel gauges* indicate the rate at which fuel is being used and the amount of fuel left in the fuel tanks.

All of these instruments are usually found even in a small, single-engine plane. An airliner has many more instruments which give the pilots, engineer, and navigator a greater amount of information about the condition of their plane (Fig. 93).

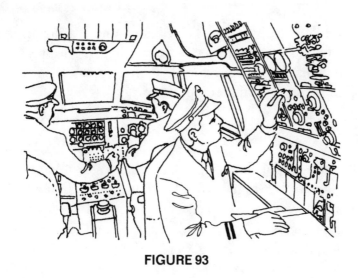

FIGURE 93

THE FORCES OF FLIGHT

When an airplane is in flight, four forces are acting upon it (Fig. 94). Gravity is pulling the plane straight down toward the ground. The *lift* of

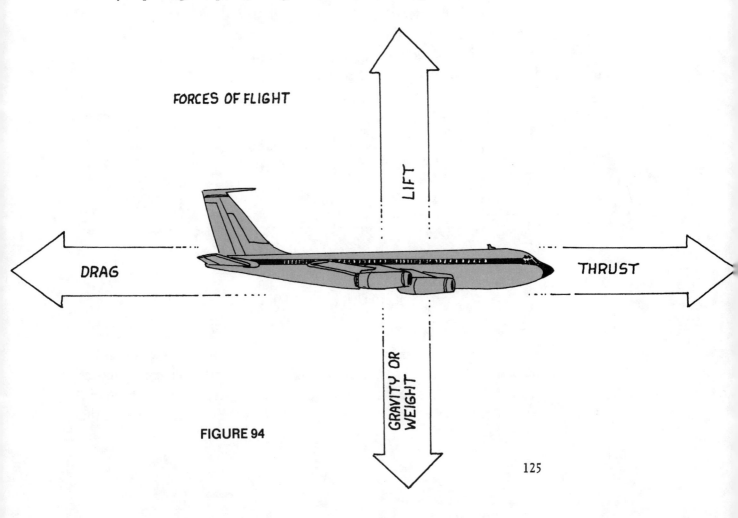

FORCES OF FLIGHT

LIFT

DRAG

THRUST

GRAVITY OR WEIGHT

FIGURE 94

the wings is pulling the plane up. The engine is moving the plane forward, creating a force called *thrust*. The air is resisting the forward motion of the plane, pulling back against thrust, with a force called *drag*. Let us examine each of the four forces separately.

GRAVITY

Gravity is the pull of the earth on any object near its surface. Gravity is the force that makes things fall. Anything that falls is being pulled down by gravity. The force of gravity is measured in units of weight: ounces, grams, pounds, kilograms, tons, etc. Thus, the force of gravity acting on an airplane is equal to the weight of the plane.

LIFT

Lift is produced by two things: (1) the shape of the airplane's wing and (2) thrust. Lift and thrust work together.

To understand lift, we must know a principle in physics discovered more than two hundred years ago by a Swiss mathematician and physicist, Daniel Bernoulli. He found that when the speed of a moving fluid is high, the pressure of the fluid is low; and when the speed is low, the pressure is high (Fig. 95). Although air is a mixture of gases, it acts as a fluid, so this discovery applies to air.

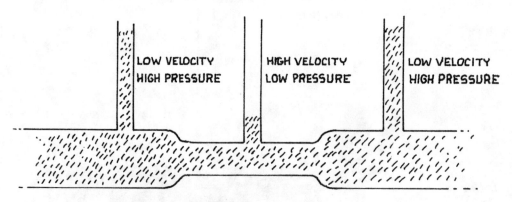

BERNOULLI'S PRINCIPLE
FIGURE 95

Have you ever noticed how a shower curtain moves inward toward the spray of water? The water moving out of the shower nozzle moves air along with it. The swiftly moving air decreases the pressure on the inside of the shower curtain and the pressure of the outside air pushes the curtain inward.

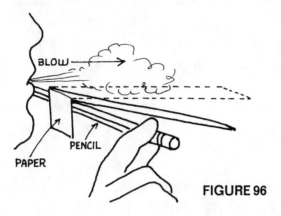

BLOW

PENCIL

PAPER

FIGURE 96

Bend one end of a short strip of paper around a pencil. Hold the pencil near your lips and blow your breath across it (Fig. 96). The paper will rise and remain extended in the air as long as you continue to blow. The fast-moving air from your lips lessens the air pressure above the paper and the higher pressure of the air beneath pushes the paper upward.

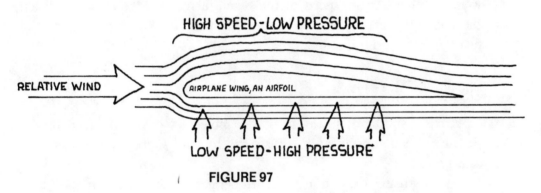

HIGH SPEED-LOW PRESSURE

RELATIVE WIND

AIRPLANE WING, AN AIRFOIL

LOW SPEED-HIGH PRESSURE

FIGURE 97

An airplane wing is flat on the bottom and curved on the top (Fig. 97). The curved surface is longer than the flat one. Air flowing across the top of the wing must therefore pass over the curve in the same time that air flows along the straight undersurface. Since air moving across the upper surface must travel a longer distance in the same length of time, this air must move faster. The faster movement of air across the upper surface causes the air pressure on the top of the wing to be less than the pressure on the bottom. This is what we would expect, according to Bernoulli's Principle. The greater pressure beneath the wing pushes it upward.

Lift is increased by the flap on the trailing edge of a wing. The flap increases the curved area of the wing. If you watch a large airplane taking off, you probably will see the pilot lower the flaps as the plane gains speed on the runway.

THRUST

An airplane may be pulled or pushed through the air by a propeller. Or, an airplane is moved through the air by a jet or rocket engine. A propeller, a jet engine, and a rocket work on the same force principle, which is called *reaction*. This is the same force that causes a rowboat to move *away* from a dock as you jump off the boat *toward* the dock.

Because the blades of an airplane propeller are shaped like airfoils, their movement through the air creates a low-pressure area in front of the propeller and a high-pressure area behind. The result is to "grab" the air in front and push it toward the rear with greatly increased speed. The reaction to the backward push of air moves the plane forward.

Jet and rocket engines push a great amount of gas rearward at very high speed, and the reaction to the backward push moves the plane forward. Thus, for an airplane, the reaction force creates thrust.

The moment an airplane on an airport runway begins to move forward, lift begins to pull upward on the wings. This is how lift and thrust work together. As the speed of the plane increases, lift increases. When the increasing lift force becomes greater than the force of gravity, the plane rises from the ground.

DRAG

Air is a substance made up of the molecules of a number of gases. Because it is a substance, air resists the forward motion of an airplane, causing drag.

As air streams past an airplane, the effect is the same as if the plane were standing still and the air were flowing past it. This air flow is called *relative wind*.

Air directly in front of an airplane wing parts and flows over and under the wing (Fig. 98). The air flowing in contact with the upper

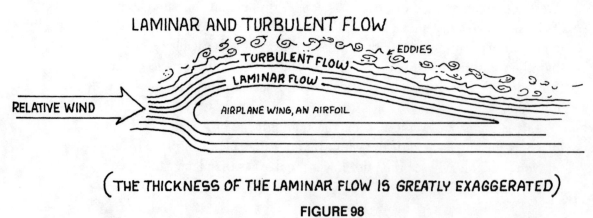

LAMINAR AND TURBULENT FLOW

EDDIES

TURBULENT FLOW

LAMINAR FLOW

RELATIVE WIND

AIRPLANE WING, AN AIRFOIL

(THE THICKNESS OF THE LAMINAR FLOW IS GREATLY EXAGGERATED)

FIGURE 98

surface is called the *boundary layer*. It moves slower than the air directly above. The boundary layer is quite shallow. On a large wing, it is as deep as thick cardboard. As the plane flies faster, the boundary layer becomes thicker. At moderate speeds, air in the boundary layer flows over the wing as if the air were made up of sheets. This is called *laminar flow* and is a smooth flow. The bottom of the layer does not move at all, while the uppermost part may move at hundreds of miles per hour. As the speed of the plane increases, and the boundary layer becomes thicker, the upper part breaks up into whirlpools of air called *eddies*. This creates a choppy flow called *turbulence*, which greatly increases drag and lessens lift. Slowly turn on the water in a faucet. As the individual drops first make a single stream, it is a smooth, clear column of water, which is an example of laminar flow (Fig. 99). Continue to open the faucet slowly.

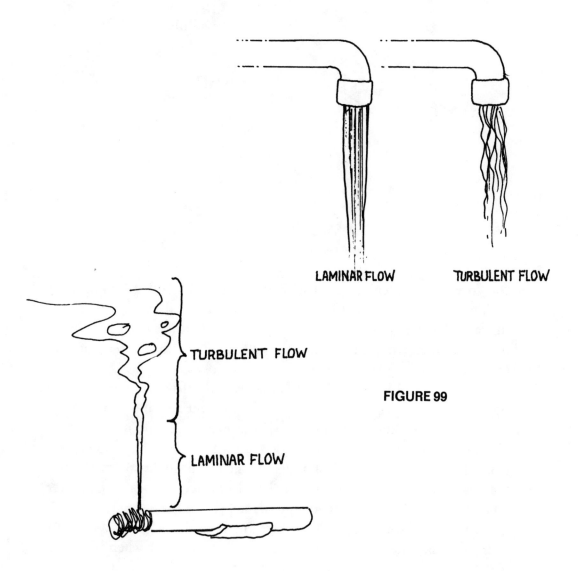

LAMINAR FLOW   TURBULENT FLOW

TURBULENT FLOW

LAMINAR FLOW

FIGURE 99

For a while, the water continues its laminar flow. Then the smooth stream develops ridges and begins to twist, picking up air to give it a murky look. This is *turbulent flow*. Another example of laminar and turbulent flow is smoke arising in still air from a cigarette in an ashtray (Fig. 99). At first the smoke rises in continuous streams of laminar flow; then it begins to zigzag and breaks up into eddies of turbulent flow.

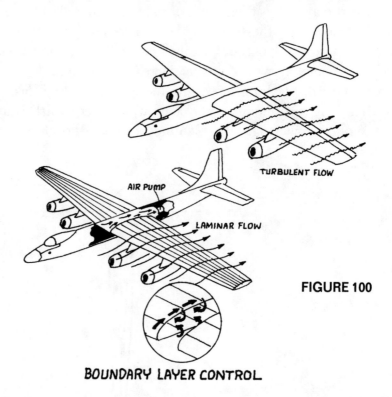

TURBULENT FLOW

AIR PUMP

LAMINAR FLOW

FIGURE 100

BOUNDARY LAYER CONTROL

To avoid turbulence, a wing may have rows of holes that lead to tubes within the wing (Fig. 100).The tubes, in turn, lead to pumps in the fuselage. These pull in air through the holes in the wing and pump it out the rear of the plane. The air pulled into the wings prevents the build-up of a thick boundary layer and the eddies that follow.

Since it is laminar flow of the boundary layer that maintains lift, the boundary layer must remain intact all the time an airplane is in the air. This becomes especially important when a plane is climbing. As an airplane climbs, its wings form an angle with a line parallel to the ground (Fig. 101). This is the angle of attack. If the plane climbs so steeply that the angle of attack becomes greater than 15 degrees, the boundary layer separates from the wing. Lift disappears and the airplane stalls. Then it falls, nose first, spinning as it goes down. It is difficult for a pilot to bring his plane out of a spin. If he is flying at low altitude when his plane

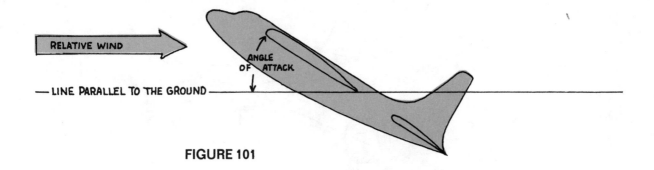

RELATIVE WIND

ANGLE OF ATTACK

— LINE PARALLEL TO THE GROUND —

FIGURE 101

begins to spin, he probably will not have time enough to get out of the spin and will crash.

If a slot is built into the upper surface of the wing near the leading edge, air will continue to flow smoothly over the wing, even though the angle of attack is a few degrees over 15.

STREAMLINING

The wings of an airplane are not the only parts that cause drag. Every other part exposed to the air rushing past the plane contributes to drag. Drag on all outer parts of an airplane is combatted by *streamlining*. This is the design of airplane structures so that air will flow past them with laminar flow, or at least with very little turbulence (Fig. 102). Streamlining cuts down on the amount of thrust needed to move a plane. This means that smaller and lighter engines can be used and fuel will be saved.

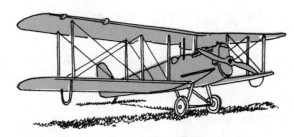

WORLD WAR I PLANE—NOT STREAMLINED

STREAMLINED MODERN PLANE

FIGURE 102

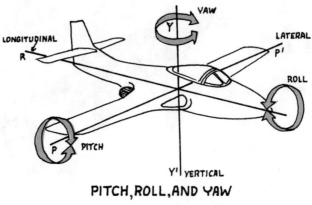

PITCH, ROLL, AND YAW

FIGURE 103

PITCH, ROLL, AND YAW

An airplane can move in three main pairs of directions. Imagine three straight lines, each one perpendicular to the other two, meeting at a single point within an airplane (Fig. 103). Each line is an *axis*. Two of these, P-P′ and R-R′, are parallel to the ground, and Y-Y′ is perpendicular to the ground.

When an airplane dives or climbs, it turns down or up around P-P′. A turn in either of this pair of directions is a *pitch*. When a plane dips either wing, so as to turn around axis R-R′, the turn is a *roll*. When a plane flies to the right or left, turning around Y-Y′, the turn is a *yaw*.

THE AIRPLANE IN FLIGHT

Having seen how the separate parts of an airplane work, let us now see how they work together when an airplane is in flight. We will use a small plane for our example.

With his airplane on an airport parking apron, a pilot asks the control tower for instructions on when to take off and what runway to use. He will be told to use a runway on which his airplane can face into the wind. The reason for this is that the wind blowing past the plane adds its speed to the speed given the plane by the thrust of the engine. This increases lift. Once he begins to move down the runway, the pilot opens the throttle all the way. This causes the engine to run at full power and gives as much thrust as the engine can produce. The pilot makes sure that the elevators are in neutral (horizontal) position, and he lowers the wing flaps a little way. His plane moves down the runway, gaining speed.

132

When the relative wind has reached a little more than 40 miles per hour, the wings provide enough lift to raise the nose off the ground. The pilot lowers the flaps all the way to give more lift to the wings. Keeping the engine at full power, he pulls the yoke (or stick) all the way toward himself. This raises the elevators all the way. The force of the relative wind streaming past the plane pushes on the elevators, holding the tail down. The wings continue to lift the forward part of the fuselage, and the whole plane rises off the ground.

Once the plane is in the air, the pilot raises the wing flaps almost all the way up. He pushes the yoke halfway forward, lowering the elevators so that they are only halfway up. He does this because he does not want the plane to climb at too steep an angle and stall.

With his plane safely in the air, the pilot climbs to flying altitude. He keeps the throttle wide open, the elevators still halfway up, and he puts the flaps in neutral position—in line with the wings.

Once he is at the altitude he wants, the pilot puts his plane in position to cruise. He lowers the elevators to neutral to end the plane's climb. He partly closes the throttle, cutting down the engine's power and with it the thrust. He is now ready to put the plane on course.

If the pilot wants to turn to the left, he pushes down on the left rudder pedal, which turns the rudder to the left. The relative wind pushes on the rudder and yaws the tail to the right, heading the nose to the left (Fig. 104). If the pilot does nothing more than push on the left rudder pedal, the whole plane will slide to the left in a *skid*, and then continue in the same direction in which it was flying. So, when the pilot pushes on the left pedal, he also turns the yoke (or moves the stick) to

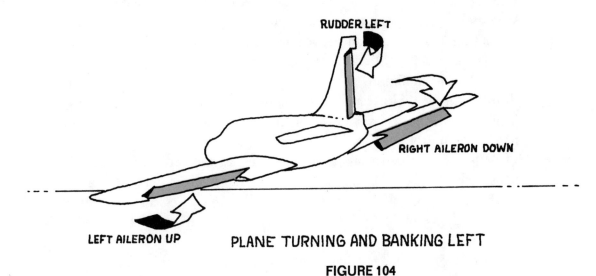

RUDDER LEFT

RIGHT AILERON DOWN

LEFT AILERON UP   PLANE TURNING AND BANKING LEFT

FIGURE 104

the left. This raises the left aileron and lowers the right one. The force of the relative wind pushes the left wing down and raises the right one. This rolls the plane toward the left. The left roll, combined with the left yaw, smoothly turns the plane left in a maneuver called a *bank*. (When you ride a bicycle around a turn, you lean in the direction of the turn; this banks the bicycle.) A banking airplane is like a racing car going around a curve at high speed. If the race track is not slanted upward (banked) at the curve, the car will turn sideways and skid in the same direction it was traveling before it reached the turn. If a pilot banks his plane too steeply, it will *slip*—or pull farther around then he wishes to turn.

Banking a plane causes it to lose thrust and tend to head downward. To keep the plane in level flight, the pilot opens the throttle a small amount to increase thrust. He also pulls back on the yoke to increase the angle of attack. The pilot does these things as he is banking, so as to have a smooth turn.

Once the pilot has the plane at the altitude he wants and pointed in the right direction, and if the air is fairly calm, he adjusts the throttle to provide the power needed for the speed he wants. He also sets *trim tabs*. These are small flaps on the tail and wings. The tabs automatically compensate for small forces that act to change the plane's direction and altitude. These forces are crosswinds and small updrafts and downdrafts of air. Also, as fuel empties from one wing tank, the plane becomes lighter on the side in which the tank is located. An adjustment must be made to keep the plane from tipping to the side with the full tank. The trim tabs make this adjustment automatically. Once the pilot has set his controls, he can fly "hands off." This means he does not continually have to steer and adjust the throttle. He can give some time to navigation—working out on a chart the plane's overland course.

Having reached his destination, the pilot makes ready to land his plane. With the airport in sight, he partly closes the throttle, reducing thrust and speed. He keeps the elevators in neutral. He lowers the wing flaps. Because he has cut down on thrust, he loses some lift, and the flaps make up for the loss.

When close to the airport, the pilot closes the throttle farther. He pulls back a little on the yoke, raising the elevators slightly. This keeps the tail from going up as the nose sinks down due to the lessening of thrust. As a result, the plane remains in level flight, gliding, rather than diving downward.

When the pilot judges that his plane has reached a point from which it can glide down to the landing strip, he closes the throttle almost all the way, nearly cutting off the engine. This lessens thrust very much, so the pilot pulls the yoke almost all the way back, further raising the elevators. And he keeps the wing flaps down. This part of the landing is the *flareout*.

When the plane's wheels touch down on the landing strip, the pilot keeps the elevators up, so that the plane touches down still in level position. He may also pull the flaps up. Finally, the pilot puts on the brakes to bring the plane to a halt.

GLIDER

A glider is an engineless airplane. But gliders are as much "soarers" as they are "gliders." They soar up and glide down. Almost all gliders are flown for fun. Most carry no more than two persons, although large passenger- and cargo-carrying gliders have been built and flown.

A glider has a longer wingspan than an airplane with a fuselage of the same length, because the glider must get as much lift as possible from its slower speed. Most gliders are *sailplanes* (Fig. 105-A and -B). They have enclosed cockpits and their wings are long and may be tapered.

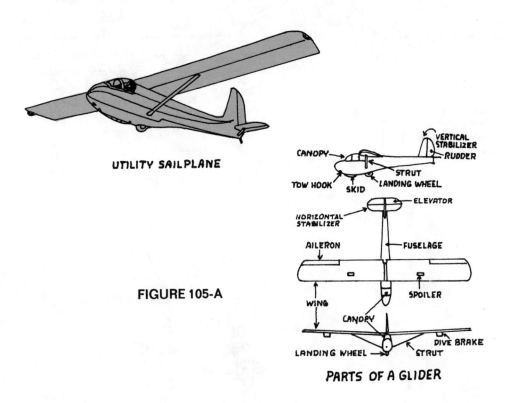

UTILITY SAILPLANE

FIGURE 105-A

PARTS OF A GLIDER

HIGH PERFORMANCE SAILPLANE
FIGURE 105-B

Some gliders do have engines. The aircraft carrying these engines are called gliders rather than airplanes because the engines are used only for taking off and gaining altitude, not as a way of providing thrust for flying.

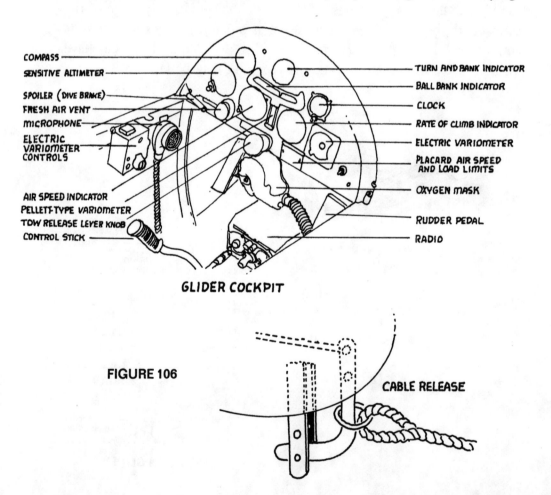

COMPASS
SENSITIVE ALTIMETER
SPOILER (DIVE BRAKE)
FRESH AIR VENT
MICROPHONE
ELECTRIC VARIOMETER CONTROLS

TURN AND BANK INDICATOR
BALL BANK INDICATOR
CLOCK
RATE OF CLIMB INDICATOR
ELECTRIC VARIOMETER
PLACARD AIR SPEED AND LOAD LIMITS

AIR SPEED INDICATOR
PELLETT-TYPE VARIOMETER
TOW RELEASE LEVER KNOB
CONTROL STICK

OXYGEN MASK
RUDDER PEDAL
RADIO

GLIDER COCKPIT

FIGURE 106

CABLE RELEASE

A glider has a control stick and rudder pedals (Fig. 106). At the pilot's left hand is a lever for raising and lowering *spoilers* and *dive brakes*. Spoilers are long narrow plates that can be raised from the upper surfaces of the wings to increase drag and lessen speed (Fig. 105-A). Dive brakes resemble spoilers, but they project downward from the undersides of the wings. Also, in the cockpit of a glider, there is a tow-release lever for releasing a towing cable which is attached to the glider's nose by a *cable release* (Fig. 106). This device is a hinged hook that fits securely into a catch. When the pilot pulls on the cable-release lever, the catch opens, the hook swings down, and the end of the cable falls out.

The instruments in the cockpit of a glider vary from glider to glider. Among them may be a magnetic compass, a turn-and-bank indicator, a ball bank indicator (which indicates the degree of banking in a turn), an accelerometer (for measuring gains or losses in speed in terms of gravities), an air-speed indicator, and one or two variometers (very sensitive barometers that measure changes in air pressure). There usually is a two-way radio for communicating with glider crews on the ground.

The landing gear of most sailplanes consists of a single wheel and two skids. The wheel is mounted at the bottom of the fuselage. The axle of the wheel is at the lower surface of the fuselage, so that half the wheel is inside and half is outside the fuselage. A brake operated by the pilot slows down the wheel when the glider is landing. One skid is in front of the wheel and one is under the tail.

LAUNCHING

Since most gliders have no engines to pull them into the air, they must be launched into flight by other means (Fig. 107). The simplest is the *shoulder launch*. A number of people hoist the glider upon their shoulders and run with it against the wind until it is airborne. This must be done on a gently sloping hill where the lift of the glider's wings can begin to act almost immediately. Another method that works in hilly country is the *bungee launch*. A bungee is a long elastic rope. A strong hook that opens downward and to the rear is affixed to the nose of the glider, and the middle of the bungee is slipped into the hook. The tail of the glider is held firmly by two men, while six or eight others—half of them grasping each end of the bungee—walk downhill. This stretches the bungee into a V, with the glider in the middle, at the crotch. When the pull of the stretched bungee becomes too strong for the two men at the tail, they let go. The bungee snaps forward, giving the glider enough speed to lift into the air. When the glider sails past the line of walkers, the bungee slips off the

137

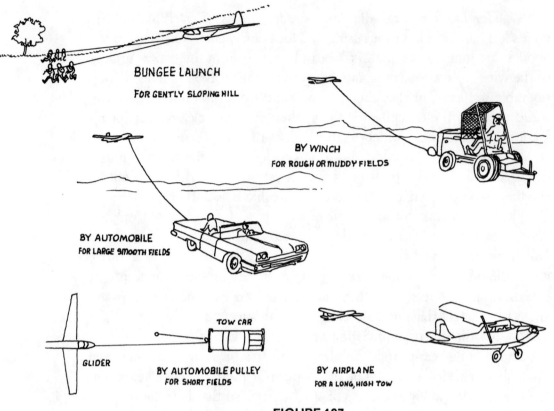

BUNGEE LAUNCH
FOR GENTLY SLOPING HILL

BY WINCH
FOR ROUGH OR MUDDY FIELDS

BY AUTOMOBILE
FOR LARGE SMOOTH FIELDS

GLIDER
TOW CAR
BY AUTOMOBILE PULLEY
FOR SHORT FIELDS

BY AIRPLANE
FOR A LONG, HIGH TOW

FIGURE 107

hook and falls to the ground. A bungee launching is like launching a small model airplane with a rubber-band slingshot.

A third way of launching a glider is to tow it with a *winch*. This is a large metal drum which is turned by an engine. One end of a long wire cable is attached to the drum. The other end is attached to the glider by means of a cable release on the glider's nose. The glider is pointed into the wind and the winch begins to turn, winding the cable on the sides of the drum. The glider is towed toward the drum at speeds of 20 to 60 miles per hour. The towed glider lifts into the air and sails over the winch. The cable release opens automatically, detaching the cable from the glider. Near the upper end of the cable, a small parachute opens and slows the fall of the cable to the ground.

The most common way of launching a glider is by towing it behind an automobile or airplane. This kind of launch requires a few acres of flat ground. If the towing vehicle is an automobile, an 800- to 1,000-foot wire cable or nylon rope is used. The automobile accelerates from a standstill to as much as 60 miles per hour. If the towing vehicle is an airplane, a shorter tow rope about 200 feet long is used.

SOARING AND GLIDING

Gliders soar on *updrafts*, which are rising currents of air, and they glide forward in still air or on winds, which are currents of air moving parallel to the ground. As they glide, they slowly sink toward the earth, being pulled down by the force of gravity. Sometimes a glider may sink very rapidly if it is caught in a *downdraft*, which is a current of falling air.

Ridge soaring is riding a glider on updrafts that form when winds are turned upward as they blow against the sides of ridges, hills, mountains, or cliffs (Fig. 108-A).

Another kind of updraft is found over bare or newly plowed fields, sandy beaches, paved roads, and shopping centers. These areas absorb and radiate much of the heat that they receive from the sun, or they simply reflect the sun's heat. This heats the air directly above the ground, and the heated air is pushed upward by the surrounding cooler air. Thus, updrafts are formed. Because these updrafts are due to the action of

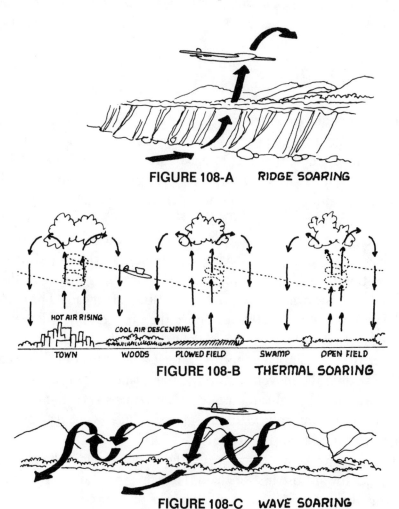

FIGURE 108-A   RIDGE SOARING

HOT AIR RISING

COOL AIR DESCENDING

TOWN   WOODS   PLOWED FIELD   SWAMP   OPEN FIELD

FIGURE 108-B   THERMAL SOARING

FIGURE 108-C   WAVE SOARING

heat, they are called *thermals*. Riding upon them is called *thermal soaring* (Fig. 108-B). Thermals are also found beneath woolly cumulus clouds; indeed, cumulus clouds form as warm moist air spirals upward and the moisture condenses.

Downdrafts are found over rivers, lakes, forests, fields with tall crops, and other areas that do not return the sun's heat to the upper air very well. These areas are cooler than the air directly above them.

Glider pilots have discovered that, where winds rise over the sides of not-very-steep mountains, the winds continue over the tops of the mountains and do not fall all the way down into the valley on the other side. Instead, the winds dip downward and then rise and dip in a series of waves above the valley (Fig. 108-C). Riding upon these waves is called *wave soaring*.

A skillful glider pilot can keep his craft in the air for many hours and travel long distances. Gliders usually fly at fairly low altitudes, compared to airplanes, but gliders can soar quite high. The glider altitude record is eight miles.

PILOTING A GLIDER

A glider is about to be launched by an airplane tow. The pilot closes the plastic canopy over the cockpit, puts the controls in neutral position, and checks the cable-release lever to make sure the release is locked. Then, using his radio, he signals the airplane pilot that the glider is ready to take off. The plane begins to roll down the runway, gaining speed as it moves, and towing the glider. Before the plane is in the air, the glider lifts off the ground, because its wings provide greater lift than those of the airplane. Also, the glider, having no engine, is lighter, and lift force overcomes the force of gravity more easily. Once his glider is in the air, the pilot keeps the wings level and steers straight ahead. The airplane tows the glider to about 2,000 feet above the ground. The glider pilot is having a bumpy ride because he is sailing through the turbulent back-wash of air from the airplane, but he can get a good idea of flying conditions by watching the movements of the tow plane. When he is ready to fly alone, he pulls the cable-release lever. He waits to see the end of the towline spring forward ahead of his glider. Then he banks the glider, turning to get away from the plane's backwash.

The glider pilot knows where he can find updrafts near the gliderport, and he glides toward the first of them. He gains some altitude by soaring upward on thermals rising over a few acres of plowed fields. Then he glides to where he can ridge soar over a group of nearby hills. Once over the hills, he watches his variometer, seeking out waves of rising air in the valley beyond the hills. Gliding now a little to the right, now to the left, he navigates into the rising air. It is a warm, sunny afternoon, and cumulus clouds are forming, some building up to thunderclouds. This means that there are strong thermals beneath the clouds. Heading for a cloud, the pilot soars to 8,000 feet. Since there are many cumulus clouds, the pilot can find plenty of thermals, and he can spend all afternoon soaring in them if he wishes. However, he must be careful not to get caught in the severe updrafts of an actual thundercloud.

When he has finished soaring and has returned to the neighborhood of the gliderport, the pilot makes his approach, flareout, and touchdown much as an airplane pilot does, except that he has no throttle to regulate. When the glider touches down on the runway, the pilot slows it with the landing-wheel brake, causing the tail to touch the ground and ride on the tail skid.

ROTORS: TANDEM, THREE BLADED
LANDING GEAR: THREE WHEELS

ROTORS: TWO BLADED COUNTER ROTATING TWIN SHAFTS.
LANDING GEAR: WHEELS.

ROTORS: TRIPLE TANDEM, THREE BLADED
LANDING GEAR: WHEELS

ROTORS: TWO BLADED COUNTER ROTATING
SINGLE SHAFT.

LANDING GEAR: SKIDS AND WHEELS

ROTOR-THREE BLADED-LANDING GEAR
RUBBER BALLOON TIRES

ROTOR-TWO BLADE JET TIPPED
LANDING GEAR-WHEELS

ROTOR-TWO BLADED-LANDING GEAR-SKIDS + WHEELS

HELICOPTER

A helicopter is an aircraft with moving wings. It can fly straight up and down, forward and backward, sidewise, and in any angle between these directions. And, probably most important, it can fly very slowly or hover over one spot.

A helicopter may have two to six wings (Fig. 109), which are long and

ROTOR-FOUR BLADED-LANDING GEAR
SKIDS AND WHEELS

FIGURE 109

141

narrow and are attached to a central hub. The wings, called *blades*, rotate around a central hub which is attached to the drive shaft of the engine. A cross section of a helicopter blade is shaped like a cross section of an airplane wing; the blade is an airfoil. This shape produces a lift force when the blades move through the air. The blades and hub make up a *rotary wing*, or *rotor*. On most helicopters, the blades range between 20 and 40 feet long, and are attached to the hub by horizontal hinges (Fig. 110) which allow them to "flap," or move up and down, as they whirl around. They also are attached by vertical hinges which allow them to "lead and lag," or move forward and backward, from a straight-out position. And the blades can be "feathered," or have their pitch (angle with the horizontal) varied. Very long blades, those of 80 to 100 feet, are not attached by hinges. They can flap and lead and lag because their great length allows them to bend.

The fuselages of helicopters are constructed in many shapes (Fig. 109). Each is suited to a different purpose, such as carrying passengers or cargo; lifting loads; aerial rescue work; carrying troops, attacking, patrolling, and observing in warfare; and others.

The landing gear of helicopters (Fig. 109) may consist of skids or wheels, or both, on the same helicopter. Some have two large rubber cylinders attached to the fuselage by struts. This kind of landing gear enables a helicopter to take off and land on many different surfaces, such as land, water, snow, ice, and marshland.

A helicopter has no rudder or elevators. At the rear end of the fuselage is a small, two-, three-, or four-bladed variable-pitch propeller that faces sideways. It is the *tail rotor*. It is on the side away from which the main rotor blades are moving as they pass the rear of the fuselage (Fig. 110). This usually is the left side. The tail rotor produces yaw for steering the helicopter. On the other side of the tail section, opposite the rotor, is a horizontal stabilizer.

The reaction to the spinning blades of a helicopter's main rotor produces a force called *torque* which tends to spin the fuselage in the direction opposite that toward which the main rotor blades are turning. To keep torque from spinning the fuselage of a single-rotor helicopter, the tail rotor pulls the tail in the direction opposite to torque. With the pull of the tail rotor exactly balancing torque, the rear of the helicopter does not turn (yaw) at all. The push of the tail rotor is made stronger or weaker by increasing or decreasing the pitch of the blades. This is done by connecting the pitch-changing gears in the hub of the tail rotor to two pedals in the cockpit. The left pedal increases the pitch; the right pedal decreases it.

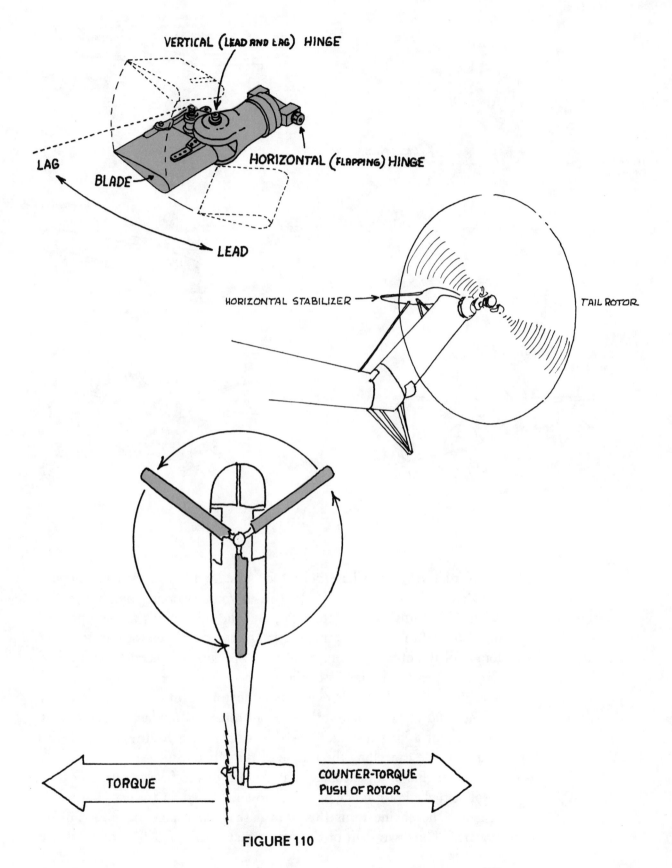

VERTICAL (LEAD AND LAG) HINGE

LAG

BLADE

HORIZONTAL (FLAPPING) HINGE

LEAD

HORIZONTAL STABILIZER

TAIL ROTOR

TORQUE

COUNTER-TORQUE
PUSH OF ROTOR

FIGURE 110

143

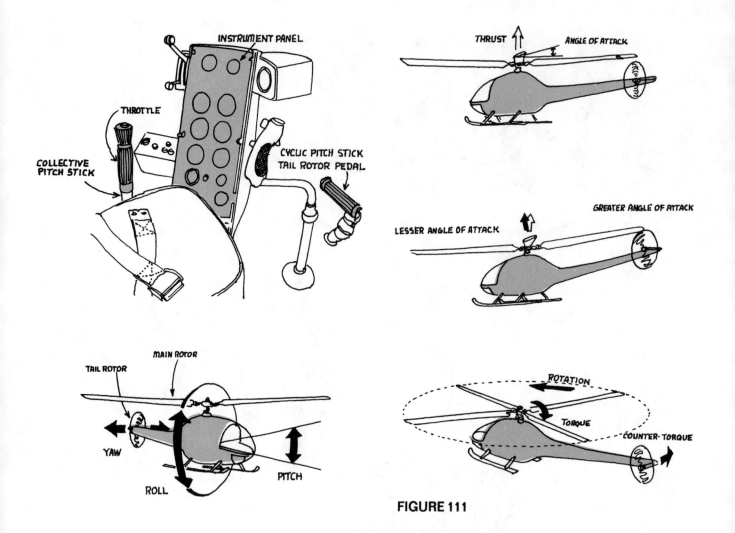

INSTRUMENT PANEL

THROTTLE

COLLECTIVE PITCH STICK

CYCLIC PITCH STICK
TAIL ROTOR PEDAL

THRUST

ANGLE OF ATTACK

LESSER ANGLE OF ATTACK

GREATER ANGLE OF ATTACK

TAIL ROTOR

MAIN ROTOR

YAW

ROLL

PITCH

ROTATION

TORQUE

COUNTER-TORQUE

FIGURE 111

Not all helicopters have tail rotors. One kind that does not has *counterrotating rotors* (Fig. 109), two main rotors working one above the other. One turns from left to right; and the other turns in the opposite direction. With such an arrangement, the torque of one rotor cancels the torque of the other. When a pilot wants to turn a helicopter with counterrotating rotors, he increases the speed of one rotor, causing it to produce more torque, which overcomes the torque of the other rotor. A second kind of helicopter without a tail rotor has *tandem rotors*, one at each end of a long fuselage. The rotors turn in opposite directions, the torque of one cancelling the torque of the other.

The engine of a helicopter is at the top of the fuselage. It may be a gasoline-fuelled piston engine or a kerosene-fuelled jet turbine. By means of gears, the engine turns the vertical shaft to which the rotor hub is attached. The drive shaft of the engine may turn at 2,800 revolutions per

144

minute, but the gears turn the rotor shaft at only 450 revolutions per minute. Some helicopters send gases from a jet turbine through pipes in the blades. The outlets for the gases face across the tips of the blades, and the reaction to the outrushing gases turns the rotor.

HELICOPTER CONTROLS

The controls of a helicopter are different from those of an airplane or glider (Fig. 111). A helicopter has two control sticks. At the pilot's left is the *collective pitch stick*, which changes the pitch angle of all the main rotor blades at the same time. A greater pitch angle results in the blades meeting the air at a greater angle of attack. This increases drag, so the pilot must increase the power going to the rotor in order to overcome the increased drag. A lesser pitch angle requires less power. To make it convenient for the pilot to change both the power and the angle of the blades at the same time, the upper few inches of the collective pitch stick consist of the throttle control. This arrangement makes it possible for the pilot to adjust both pitch and power controls with one hand. He speeds up or slows down the engine by twisting the throttle control to the right or left. This throttle twist-grip is like the one on a motorcycle.

In front of the pilot, between his legs, is the cyclic pitch stick, a control that tilts the whirling main rotor forward, backward, sideways, or any direction between. Also in front of the pilot are the two foot pedals that vary the pitch of the tail rotor.

FLYING A HELICOPTER

When a helicopter pilot is ready to take off, he sets the collective pitch stick so that the main rotor blades have zero pitch. He starts the engine which does not immediately begin to turn the rotor. The shaft that turns the rotor is disconnected from the engine by a *clutch*, which is made up of a group of gears. To start the rotors, the pilot must "put the shaft into gear," which means to connect it with the drive shaft of the engine through the clutch. He does this by moving the clutch lever with his right hand. This operation is very much like putting the axles and the drive shaft of an automobile engine into gear by moving the clutch, or gearshift, lever.

With the rotors spinning, the pilot uses his left hand to pull the collective pitch stick forward. This increases the pitch angle of the rotors. At the same time, he twists the throttle control to increase power. The helicopter lifts off its landing pad (Fig. 112). When the craft has risen to

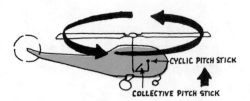

UP: All blades at same pitch and rotating fast enough to cause thrust to overcome gravity.

SIDEWAYS: Rotor tilted toward direction of travel, giving blades increased pitch as they approach side opposite direction of travel.

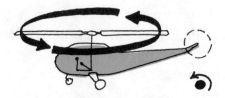

FORWARD: Rotor tilted forward, increasing pitch of blades approaching tail.

TURN: Increased pitch of tail rotor blades swings tail of craft, pointing nose in torquewise direction; or decreased pitch of tail rotor allows torque to turn craft in opposite direction.

BACKWARD: Rotor tilted backward, giving blades increased pitch as they approach the nose.

HOVER: All blades at same pitch and turning just fast enough to cause thrust to balance gravity.

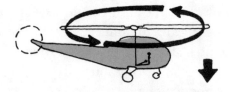

DOWN: All blades at low pitch; power almost off; relative wind spins blades.

FIGURE 112

a desired height, the pilot pushes the cyclic pitch stick forward with his right hand. This tilts the rotor forward and the helicopter moves forward.

Now, the pilot wants to turn right. He moves the cyclic pitch stick to the right and pushes the left pedal. These actions tilt the main rotor to the right and increase the pitch of the tail-rotor blades. The front of the fuselage is pulled to the right by the tilted main rotor and the rear of the fuselage is swung to the left by the tail rotor. The helicopter heads to the right. To turn left, the pilot moves the cyclic pitch stick to the left and pushes the right pedal. The main rotor is tilted to the left and the pitch of the tail-rotor blades is decreased. The front of the fuselage is pulled to the left by the tilted main rotor. The torque of this rotor overcomes the lessened pull of the tail rotor, and the rear of the fuselage is swung to the right. The helicopter heads left.

When the pilot is near his destination, he gradually moves the cyclic pitch stick toward the neutral position (straight up-and-down), cutting down forward thrust. To keep from overshooting his mark, he pulls the cyclic pitch stick past neutral, changing the forward thrust to backward thrust that slows the helicopter to a standstill. Meanwhile, the pilot cuts the throttle and pushes the collective pitch stick down. This lessens the pitch of the main rotor blades, thereby lessening lift force, and letting gravity pull the helicopter toward the ground. If the pilot does not wish to land but wants to hang motionless in the air, he uses the collective pitch stick to arrive at a balance between lift force and the force of gravity.

AIR-CUSHION VEHICLE, GROUND EFFECTS MACHINE, or HOVERCRAFT

An air-cushion vehicle is a wingless aircraft that flies or hovers only inches above the ground. It rests on a large bubble of air which is created by the shape of the fuselage and a jet of air from one or more powerful engine-driven fans. There are small air-cushion vehicles which carry one person (Fig. 113-A) and large hovercraft which carry more than two hundred passengers (Fig. 113-B).

Common sense would probably tell you that air pumped downward upon a flat surface would flow rapidly away in all directions. Instead, the downrushing air forms an outer curtain of turbulent air that surrounds and holds a large bubble of almost-stationary air (Fig. 114). This is called

FIGURE 113-A

PROPELLING FAN   AIR-CUSHION-PRODUCING FANS

FIGURE 113-B

the *ground effect*. The turbulent air continually flows rapidly outward, and some air continually leaks out of the bubble. But all the lost air is immediately replenished by the fans.

The fuselage of an air-cushion vehicle is shaped to aid in maintaining the air bubble. The simplest shape is like that of an upside-down cereal bowl (Fig. 115-A), into which air is blown through the top. Another design (Fig. 115-B), has curtains of flexible material, such as heavy canvas or plastic, that guide the air to the edges of the bubble. The pressure of the air holds the curtains, or skirts, outward. Still another type has two or three ring-shaped hollows (Fig. 115-C). Air blown into the inner ring is circulated around it by fans. Air escaping from this ring is pushed by its own pressure into the next outward ring. Here the air is again circulated by fans until it escapes to the outer ring, where it is again circulated until it escapes from the vehicle altogether. The pressure of the air increases from ring to ring, being highest in the outer ring.

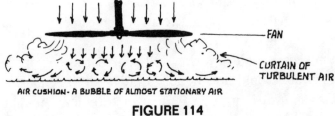

FAN

CURTAIN OF TURBULENT AIR

AIR CUSHION- A BUBBLE OF ALMOST STATIONARY AIR

FIGURE 114

148

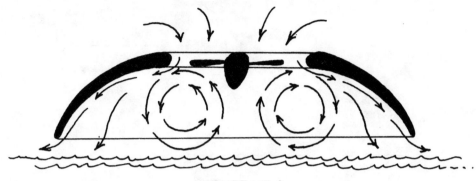

FIGURE 115-A

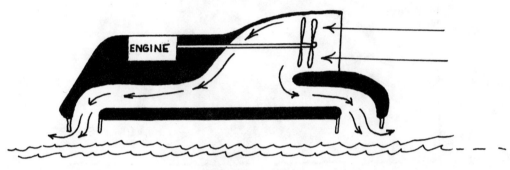

FIGURE 115-B

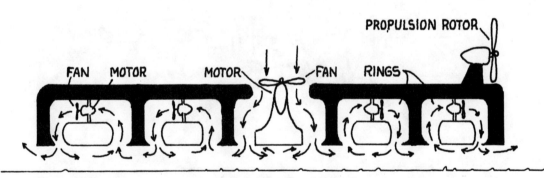

FIGURE 115-C

An air-cushion vehicle can be propelled in any horizontal direction—forward, backward, to either side, or any angle in between. Propulsion is accomplished in several ways (Fig. 116): (1) horizontal nozzles use some of the high-pressure air to form propelling jets. (2) The vehicle is tilted by increasing the pressure in air jets on one side and lessening it on the other. The jets push the vehicle toward the lower side. (3) The inlet for the main fan is pointed in the direction the vehicle is to move. A low-

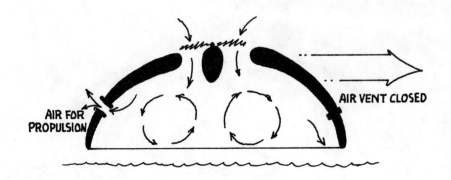

AIR FOR PROPULSION

AIR VENT CLOSED

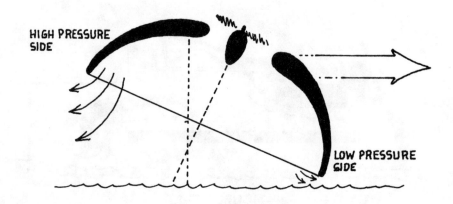

HIGH PRESSURE SIDE

LOW PRESSURE SIDE

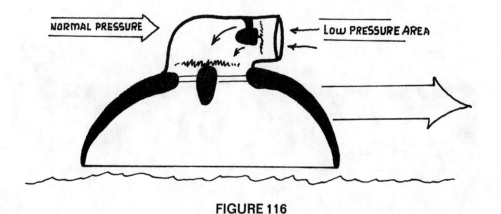

NORMAL PRESSURE

LOW PRESSURE AREA

FIGURE 116

pressure area is formed in front of the inlet and the vehicle is pushed into this area by normal atmospheric pressure behind. (4) Large air-cushion vehicles usually have airplane-type propellers or propeller-like rotors within cylindrical housings (Fig. 113-B).

There is almost no friction between the air bubble and the surface over which an air-cushion vehicle moves. Therefore, very little power is needed to propel the vehicle. But much power is needed to form and maintain the bubble. And power is needed to overcome the drag of the moving vehicle, especially when it is moving fast. All this takes three or four times as much power as is used to move a truck of the same weight at the same speed. But it takes only one-fourth to one-half as much power as propelling an airplane or helicopter.

An air-cushion vehicle can travel over land, water, snow, ice, marshland, or any dense surface. It cannot climb over hills that rise more than five feet in every hundred feet of forward travel. Also, it cannot travel over a surface that has obstacles that are higher than the height the vehicle can rise above the ground. The highest number of inches an air-cushion vehicle can rise is one-tenth the number of feet of the length of the vehicle. For example, a vehicle that is 60 feet long can rise 6 inches.

BALLOON

A balloon is any bag filled with a gas lighter than air, so that the bag will rise. Aeronautical balloons may be used to carry useful loads—payloads—such as passengers or scientific instruments. Balloons that carry passengers usually have an open basket suspended from the gas bag (Fig. 117). Balloons that rise to very high altitudes carry passengers in completely closed spheres made of metal..The baskets, or spheres, are called *gondolas*. A balloon may float freely in the air or it may be captive, that is, tied to the ground by a rope or cable. Some balloons are driven by engines and have machinery for steering.

GAS BALLOONS

A free-floating gas balloon is spherical. Its gas bag can be made of any lightweight, strong material that is gastight—material through which gas escapes only extremely slowly. Some materials used for gas bags are rubberized cloth, specially treated paper, and polyethylene plastic. Cloth and paper gas bags are made up of a large number of triangular pieces sewn together or bonded together with adhesive.

If a balloon is to carry a heavy load, such as passengers, the gondola is suspended from a network of cords draped over the gas bag. A small circular area in the net is open at the top. The net distributes the load evenly over the surface of the gas bag so that no part of the bag has a downward-pulling strain that might tear the bag.

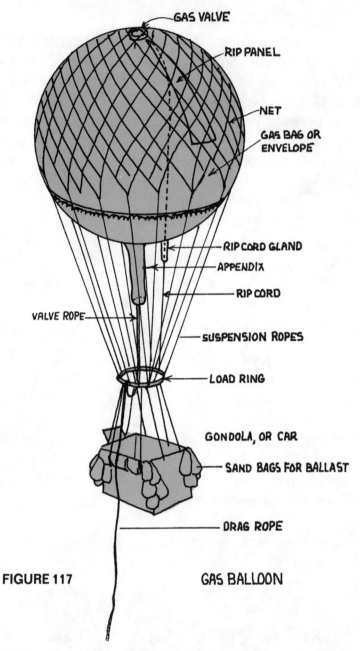

GAS VALVE

RIP PANEL

NET

GAS BAG OR ENVELOPE

RIP CORD GLAND

APPENDIX

RIP CORD

VALVE ROPE

SUSPENSION ROPES

LOAD RING

GONDOLA, OR CAR

SAND BAGS FOR BALLAST

DRAG ROPE

FIGURE 117   **GAS BALLOON**

The gondola is made of light material, such as wicker, or alloys of light metals, such as aluminum and magnesium. It usually is 5½ feet square, 3 feet high, and open at the top. It is secured to the gas bag by means of a *load ring*, which is a wooden or light-metal ring two or three feet in circumference. A large number of strong, thin ropes are spaced around the ring. They extend downward and go around all four sides of the basket, holding it securely. The gondola is suspended from the gas bag by ropes running from the load to the net.

At the bottom of the gas bag is a vertical sleeve called the *appendix*. It is used as an inlet for gas when the gas bag is being filled. Also, it is a safety valve from which gas can escape if the pressure within the gas bag becomes too great.

At the top of the gas bag is the *gas valve*, a rubber valve that ordinarily is shut tightly. It can be opened by pulling on a rope that reaches down through both the gas bag and the appendix to the gondola.

The *rip-cord gland* is similar to, but smaller than, the appendix. A strong cord—the *rip cord*—passes through the gland and gas bag and is attached to the top of the *rip panel*. It is somewhat like a zipper in the upper half of the gas bag. The rip-cord gland is separate from the appendix so that the rip cord will not tangle with the gas-valve cord. Pulling the rip cord tears open the panel and quickly lets out all the gas in the bag. Upon landing, balloonists may pull the rip cord to stop a high wind from pushing on the balloon and dragging the gondola over the ground.

The basket carries sandbags for ballast. The ballast adds weight to the basket and its contents and makes the balloon more stable, keeping it from swinging back and forth too widely. Also carried in the basket is a *drag rope*, a long heavy rope that is used in maneuvering the balloon when it is not very high above the ground.

The reason that a balloon rises in the air depends on the fact that air is fluid. The balloon is lighter than an equal volume of the surrounding air. The downward pull of gravity causes the heavier surrounding air to flow under the balloon and push it upward. The difference between the weight of the balloon and the weight of an equal volume of air is equal to the payload the balloon can carry.

HOT-AIR BALLOON

Air is a mixture of several gases. If a volume of any gas is heated, it expands and becomes lighter than an equal volume of unheated gas. So, a volume of heated air weighs less than the same volume of unheated air. This fact is used in *hot-air balloons* (Fig. 118) in which the gas bag is filled with hot air. The bag has no appendix, but is held open at the bottom by a wide ring. One or more gas-fuelled burners are suspended beneath the bag. The burners send up into the gas bag a continual flow of heated gas.

FLYING A BALLOON

Piloting a free-floating balloon is a matter of keeping the balloon at altitudes where there are winds that will push the balloon in the direction the pilot wants to fly.

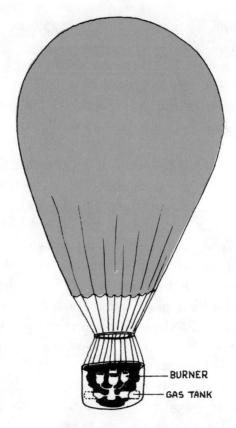

HOT AIR BALLOON

FIGURE 118

BURNER

GAS TANK

When the balloonist in flight wants to descend to a lower altitude, he pulls the gas-valve rope. This lets some gas out of the balloon and lessens its lift force. If the balloon descends too far, the balloonist can make it rise by throwing some of the sandbag ballast overboard. Being made lighter, the balloon will rise. If the balloon is maneuvering not very far above the ground, throwing the drag rope overboard will have the same effect as throwing ballast overboard. The weight of the part of the rope that is on the ground will not be pulling the balloon downward, so the balloon will be lighter by whatever the rope on the ground weighs. The drag rope is also used to slow a balloon that is sailing low over the ground.

If a balloon that is floating along in full sunlight passes beneath the clouds, the gas in the bag will cool and contract, and the balloon will lose some lift force and descend. Upon sailing back into sunlight, the gas will be warmed by the sun, and the balloon will rise. At different places in its flight, a balloon will float into currents of warm rising air or cool descending air. These will push the balloon upward and downward.

154

NON RIGID DIRIGIBLE OR BLIMP

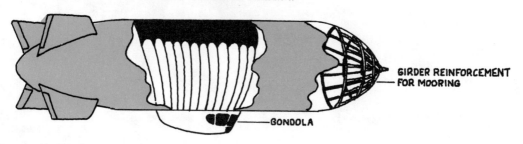

GIRDER REINFORCEMENT
FOR MOORING

GONDOLA

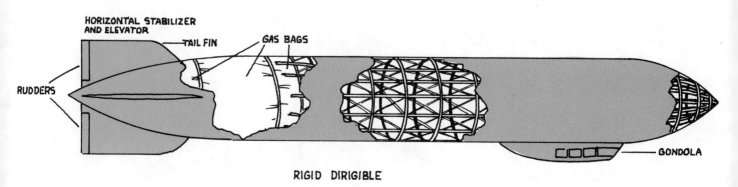

HORIZONTAL STABILIZER
AND ELEVATOR

TAIL FIN

GAS BAGS

RUDDERS

GONDOLA

RIGID DIRIGIBLE

FIGURE 119

STEERABLE BALLOON, DIRIGIBLE, OR AIRSHIP

Not all balloons are spherical. You probably have seen *blimps*, silvery, fat, cigar-shaped balloons carrying advertising signs while flying over fairgrounds or sports stadiums. These steerable balloons are one kind of *dirigible*. Their gondolas are suspended by cables that hang from the re-inforced upper part of the gas bag (Fig. 119). The largest dirigibles are rigid. They consist of several gas bags held within a framework of light-metal girders which are covered with cloth. Dirigibles are moved through the air by engine-driven propellers.

Very large dirigibles, carrying a large number of passengers and a crew, have been built. These were called *airships*. They had rigid frame-works of light-metal girders and a number of propellers. They could carry fairly heavy loads long distances at the cost of very little fuel, but they were hard to manage in high winds and were dangerously unsafe in stormy weather. The last of these airships was wrecked in a storm in 1938.

155

MEASURING TIME

Almost all measuring of time is done with watches and clocks. They work by producing a unit of motion—one swing of a pendulum, one turn of a small wheel, one back-and-forth movement of a small magnet or prong of a tuning fork. The unit of motion is then translated into the movement of second, minute, and hour hands around a dial.

WATCHES

If you want to learn what time it is by looking at a clock, you must go to where the clock is located, and you are delayed in getting that information until you arrive at the clock. On the other hand, since you can carry a watch (Fig. 120) with you wherever you go, you can always tell time instantly. This is why there are more watches than any other time-measuring instruments. Because of their smallness, watches are remarkable engineering achievements.

156

WATCH WITH SMALL SECOND HAND IN "6" POSITION

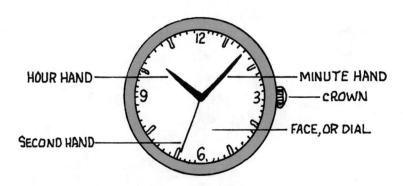

HOUR HAND — ⋅ ⋅ — MINUTE HAND
— CROWN
— FACE, OR DIAL
SECOND HAND —

WATCH WITH SWEEP SECOND HAND

FIGURE 120

MECHANICAL WATCH

To produce motion in a watch, a source of energy is needed. In *mechanical watches*, the source is a coiled spring, the *mainspring* (Fig. 121). This spring, which may be from 10 to 24 inches long, is coiled in a metal container that looks like a pillbox and is called the *barrel*. The inner end of the mainspring is attached firmly to a metal pin at the center of the barrel, while the outer end is anchored to the inner wall of the barrel. When you wind a watch, you coil the mainspring tightly and store energy in it.

To wind a watch, you turn a small knob in the side of the metal *case* that surrounds the working parts of the watch. The knob is called a *crown* (Fig. 122) and is attached to a short rod, the *stem*. Most of the length of the stem is inside the case. On the inner end of the stem is a small gear called the *winding pinion*. A pinion is a small thick gear with a small number of teeth that are designed to fit into the teeth of a larger gear. The teeth of the winding pinion fit into, or *mesh* with, the teeth of a

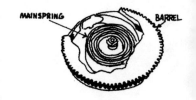

FIGURE 121

157

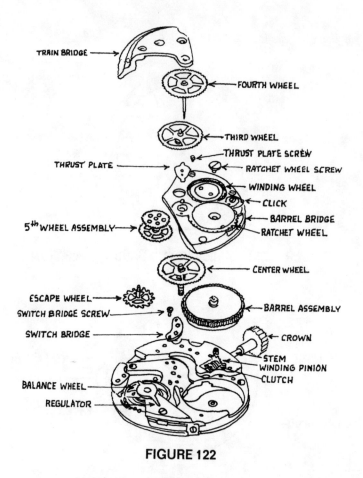

FIGURE 122

larger gear called the *winding wheel*. Finally, the winding wheel turns a toothed wheel called the *ratchet wheel*.

When the mainspring is being wound, it is always acting to unwind and turn the center pin with it. The spring is kept from unwinding by the *ratchet wheel*. This toothed wheel has a square hole in its center. The hole fits over the square top of the center pin. This assures that when the ratchet wheel turns, the pin must turn. The wheel has bevelled teeth. Another toothed wheel—a very small one with only two teeth—is located at the edge of the ratchet wheel. This little gear is called the *click* because of the sound it makes when you are winding the watch and turn the crown backward. One of the teeth of the click is slightly longer and narrower than the other. The shorter one exactly fits the space between the bevel of two teeth of the ratchet wheel. The click turns easily on a screw through its center. As you wind the watch, the longer tooth slides smoothly over the bevelled points of the ratchet wheel teeth. The click tooth is not moved completely out of the way by the turning ratchet wheel because a very small spring attached to the click holds the tooth against the ratchet wheel. As soon as you stop winding, the mainspring begins to turn the ratchet wheel in the direction opposite to the one in which you have been turning it. Immediately, the nearest tooth of the

158

ratchet wheel pushes on the longer tooth of the click. This moves the click about one-half a turn backward and jams the short tooth between two teeth of the ratchet wheel. The jammed teeth hold the ratchet wheel from turning in the direction that would unwind the mainspring.

GEAR TRAIN

With the mainspring wound, the watch has a store of energy to use. The energy must be released and made to turn the hands of the watch. This is done by allowing the mainspring to unwind slowly. Since the ratchet wheel keeps the unwinding mainspring from turning the center pin, the spring unwinds by turning the barrel to which it is anchored. The barrel makes three complete turns each 24 hours. The top of the barrel is a toothed wheel, the first wheel. As this wheel turns, its teeth mesh with the second of four gear wheels. These wheels make up the *gear train* (Fig. 123-A and -B). Each wheel is really two gears—a wide flat one and a pinion. Both are attached to a central axle called an *arbor*.

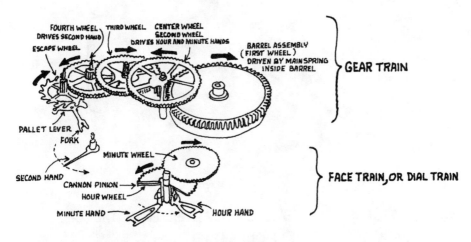

WATCH WITH SECOND HAND IN "6" POSITION ON DIAL   FIGURE 123-A

The teeth of the first wheel turn the pinion of the first geared wheel in the train, the *center wheel*, or second wheel. The barrel wheel has 8 times as many teeth as the center wheel, so the center wheel turns 8 times as fast as the barrel. This equals 24 turns per day, or one each hour. The teeth of the center wheel gear turn the pinion of the next wheel, the *third wheel*. The center wheel has 8 teeth for every 1 in the pinion of the third wheel. So, the third wheel turns one-eighth as fast as the center wheel, or one revolution every 7½ minutes. The third wheel turns the pinion of the fourth wheel, and the third wheel has 7½ teeth for every tooth of the fourth wheel pinion. So, the fourth wheel turns once every minute. This is the arrangement of the gear train in a watch that has a second hand in the "6" position on the dial (Fig. 123-A). If a watch has a sweep second hand, there is a *fifth wheel* assembly which makes it possible for the fourth wheel to be at the center of the dial (Fig. 123-B).

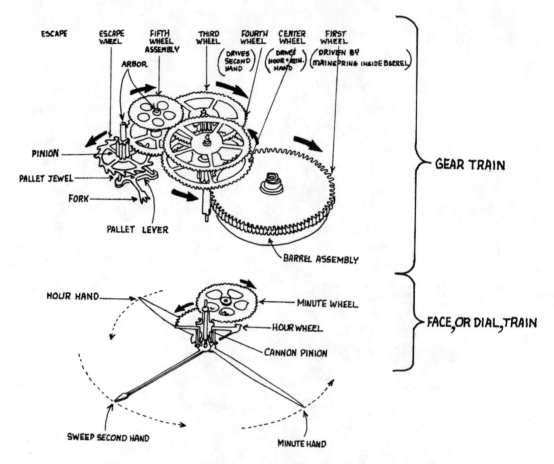

WATCH WITH SWEEP SECOND HAND AT CENTER OF THE DIAL
FIGURE 123-B

ESCAPEMENT

The fourth wheel of the gear train turns the pinion on the *escape wheel* (Fig. 124-A). In most watches, this wheel has 15 boot-shaped teeth. Next to the escape wheel is a small part shaped somewhat like an anchor with a fork at the upper end of the shank. This is the *fork and pallet*. The flukes of the anchor hold two pieces of garnet or synthetic sapphire or ruby. These are *pallet stones*, or *pallet jewels*. The *pallet lever* pivots on a *pivot bearing* halfway between the ballet jewels. Extending outward from the lever is a shank. At the free end of the shank is a small fork.

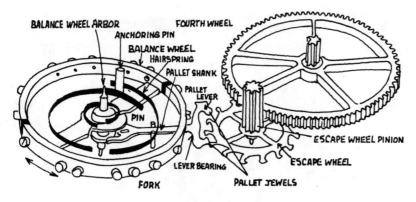

FIGURE 124-A

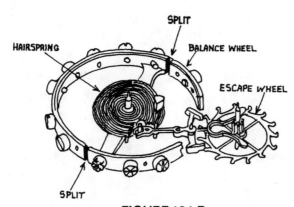

FIGURE 124-B

A fraction of an inch above the fork and pallet is the *balance wheel*. In a well-made watch, this small wheel is two half-circles attached to a wide spoke. The two splits in the wheel allow it to expand or contract without changing its shape as temperature changes. There are a number of very small screws in the rim of the wheel. The screws can be adjusted to give the balance wheel perfect balance. One end of a small, fine spring, the *hairspring,* is anchored to the arbor around which the balance wheel turns; the other end is attached to a small pin on the upper side of the spoke. On the underside of the spoke is a small triangular or half-round pin. The small fork on the shaft fits around the pin (Fig. 124-B).

Energy from the mainspring, passing through the four gears of the train, turns the escape wheel. The heel of one of the boot-shaped teeth of the wheel pushes on the inside of one pallet jewel, swinging the pallet lever a short distance around on the pivot (Fig. 125), which allows the pallet jewel to escape the tooth. The pivoting pallet lever causes the other pallet jewel to catch the heel of a tooth—the second tooth behind the one that just swung the fork. This momentarily stops the turning of the escape wheel. Meanwhile, the other end of the pivoting shaft causes the small

FIGURE 125

161

fork to push sidewise on the balance-wheel pin, turning the wheel about half a turn. The turning balance wheel winds the hairspring a little tighter. The spring immediately acts to uncoil and in doing so, turns the balance wheel in the opposite direction. The pin on the underside of the balance wheel spoke pushes the small fork back and—through the pivot—moves the pallet lever in the opposite direction, too. This frees the escape-wheel tooth held by the pallet, and allows the wheel to make one-fifth of a turn before the whole sequence of actions starts over again. This cycle of actions, which takes place five times a second, is the *escapement*. It allows energy from the mainspring to escape only in a series of short bursts. This bit-by-bit release of energy through the gear train and fork and pallet is the second way in which the wound mainspring is prevented from unwinding immediately and swiftly. (The first way was by means of the ratchet wheel.)

The escapement governs how accurately a watch keeps time. If the balance wheel turns faster than it should, all the gear wheels and the hands of the watch turn too fast. If the balance wheel turns too slowly, the watch runs slow. A watch can be regulated by moving a lever that is fixed to a part of the frame above the arbor of the balance wheel (Fig. 122). The outer end of the hairspring passes through a slot in the lower part of the lever. By moving the lever in one direction (toward the "S" for *slow*), the coil of the hairspring is loosened a little and the balance wheel moves more slowly. Moving the lever in the opposite direction (toward "F" for *fast*) tightens the coil of the spring, and the balance wheel turns faster.

JEWELS

The balance wheel of a watch swings back and forth 300 times a minute, 432,000 times a day, and almost 158 million times a year. Although the other wheels turn far fewer times, all the wheels must be able to turn without being slowed by friction enough to make the watch run slow. To cut down on friction, the ends of the wheel arbors are pointed or rounded and are mounted in circular bearings (Fig. 126). These are called jewels because they are ground from synthetic corundum, the substance of which rubies and sapphires are composed. Corundum is very hard and takes a very long time to wear down. The arbor then always has a smooth, hard surface upon which to turn. This greatly lessens friction. Also, corundum will not corrode. You may have noticed that when watches are advertised, the number of jewels is stated. In general, the more jewels (up to 23) a watch has, the better it is.

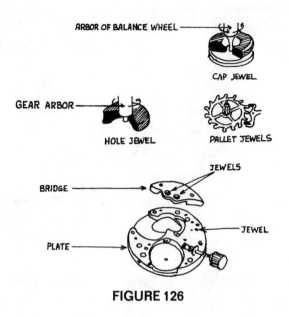

ARBOR OF BALANCE WHEEL

CAP JEWEL

GEAR ARBOR

HOLE JEWEL

PALLET JEWELS

JEWELS

BRIDGE

JEWEL

PLATE

FIGURE 126

The jewels are set into holes drilled into flat *plates* and *bridges*, which make up the *framework* of a watch.

HANDS

The arbor of the center wheel extends upward through the face of the watch and turns the *minute hand*. Near the top of this arbor (but below the face) is a pinion that turns a neighboring gear wheel called the *minute wheel* (Fig. 123). A pinion on top of the minute wheel turns a gear called the *hour wheel*. The arbor of the hour wheel is hollow. It surrounds the center-wheel arbor and extends up through the face, where the hour hand is attached to it. The hour wheel turns only one-twelfth as fast as the center wheel. Every time the center wheel turns the minute hand once around the face, the hour wheel moves one-twelfth the circumference of the face—the distance between two hour numbers. If a watch has a second hand, it may be either one that is pivoted with the other two hands at the center of the face or a small one that has a separate dial near the number "6." The first kind is a *sweep second hand*. If a watch has this kind of second hand, the arbors of both the center wheel and the hour wheel are hollow. The arbor of the hour wheel surrounds the arbor of the minute wheel, and the arbor of the gear wheel that drives the second hand passes through the arbor of the minute wheel. If the watch has a small second hand, there is an additional wheel in the gear train that turns the arbor to which the second hand is attached. All the gear wheels, pinions, and arbors that turn the hands make up the *face train* or *dial train* (Fig. 123).

163

To protect the hands of a watch, the face is covered by a *crystal*. This is a convex (outward-curving) circular glass cover. It is called a crystal because these covers used to be ground from quartz crystals.

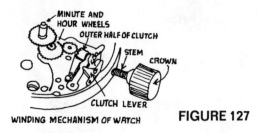

WINDING MECHANISM OF WATCH

FIGURE 127

To set the hands of a watch to the proper time, you pull on the crown, which then jumps outward a short distance. There is a clutch (Fig. 127) in the stem. When the stem is in its normal position, a gear of the clutch meshes with the winding gear. When you pull the stem out, the clutch gear disengages from the winding gear and meshes with a gear of the dial train. (The sudden opening of the clutch is what causes the crown to jump outward.) Then, when you turn the crown and stem, you turn the hour and minute hands of the watch. The springs, gear trains, escapement, and hands are called the *movement* of a watch. Figure 128 shows how the parts of the movement of a mechanical watch are arranged; however, the length of the arbor that separates the gear train from the dial train is exaggerated in order to give a clear view of all the parts.

BASIC MECHANICAL WATCH

MINUTE WHEEL
WINDING PINION
MAINSPRING
HOUR WHEEL
FOURTH WHEEL
ESCAPE WHEEL
PALLET JEWEL
PALLET
JEWEL
BALANCE WHEEL
HAIRSPRING
CROWN
CLICK
CENTER WHEEL
RACHET WHEEL
WINDING WHEEL

FIGURE 128

SELF-WINDING WATCH

A self-winding watch works the same as a finger-wound watch, but it has no crown and stem. In the lower part of the frame there is a heavy weight that turns on a pivot through its center (Fig. 129). An arbor rising

164

AUTOMATIC, OR SELF-WINDING, WATCH

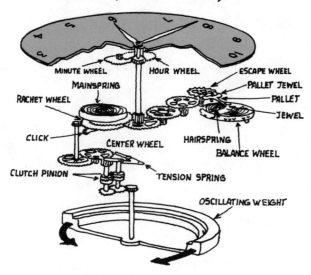

FIGURE 129

from the center of the weight has a gear at its top. This gear is connected by a train of gears and a pair of clutches to the ratchet wheel. As you carry the watch on your wrist, the motions of your arm cause the weight to turn back and forth. The clutch pinions disengage when the weight turns in one direction; they mesh when the weight turns in the opposite direction. When they are meshed, the turning of the weight turns the winding gear. Throughout a day, the weight is turned back and forth a sufficient number of times to wind the watch.

ELECTRIC WATCH

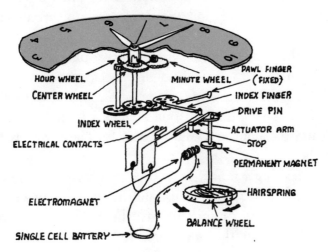

FIGURE 130

ELECTRIC WATCH

An electric watch has no mainspring (Fig. 130). Energy for running the watch comes from a tiny electric cell, or battery. Since there is no mainspring, there is no barrel, winding wheel, or ratchet wheel. Also, no fork-and-pallet escapement.

When the electrical contacts are touching, current flows from the battery to a coil of wire. This makes the coil into an *electromagnet*. The magnetic force of the electromagnet pushes upon the *permanent magnet*. This turns the *drive pin* away from the *actuator arm*, which is made of springy metal. The springiness of the actuator arm causes it to move in the same direction as the drive pin. This pulls one of the electrical contacts—the one attached to the actuator arm—away from the other contact, which is stationary. Pulling the electrical contacts apart breaks the electric circuit. With no electric current flowing through the wires, the coil no longer is an electromagnet. Then there no longer is a push on the permanent magnet. Also, the moment the electrical contact is broken, the actuator arm ends its outward movement because it hits the *stop*, which is immovable.

When the electromagnet pushes upon the permanent magnet, the arbor extending down to the balance wheel is turned. This coils the hairspring a little tighter and turns the balance wheel counterclockwise. As soon as the electrical contact is broken, the hairspring begins to uncoil and turns the balance wheel in the opposite direction—clockwise. The permanent magnet, being attached to the same arbor as the hairspring, also reverses direction. So does the drive pin.

As the drive pin turns back, it strikes the actuator arm and pushes upon it. This brings the electrical contacts together. Electric current flows from the battery again, and the whole cycle of events takes place again.

Attached to the actuator arm, near the drive pin, is a rod called the *index finger*. Each time the drive pin pushes against the actuator arm, the free end of the index finger pushes upon a tooth of the *index wheel*. The turning of this wheel is transferred by a gear train and arbors to the center wheel and the hour and minute wheels. These wheels then turn the hands of the watch.

Since the index finger moves both back and forth, it might not only push the index wheel forward, but also pull it back. To prevent this, the *pawl finger*, which is fixed immovably to the framework of the watch, acts as a ratchet. This keeps the index wheel from turning backward.

166

ELECTRONIC, OR TUNING-FORK, WATCH

An electronic watch is much like an electric one, but it does not have a balance wheel and hairspring. Also, instead of the electrical contacts and actuator arm of an electric watch, an electronic watch has an electronic circuit (Fig. 131) and a tiny fork shaped exactly like a *tuning fork*. The electronic circuit, which consists of transistors, receives current from an electric battery. The electronic circuit alternately completes and breaks the electric circuit. When the electric circuit is complete, the two electromagnets pull into the drive coils the two metal pins protruding from the sides of the prongs of the tuning fork. The *sensing coil* is part of the electronic circuit. When the pin around which this coil is wrapped enters the electromagnet, the sensing coil signals the electronic circuit—by means of a pulse of electric current—to break the electric circuit. When the electric circuit is broken, the twin coils cease to be electromagnets. And the springiness of the prongs pulls the pins out of the coils. The prongs are pulled and released 3,600 times a minute.

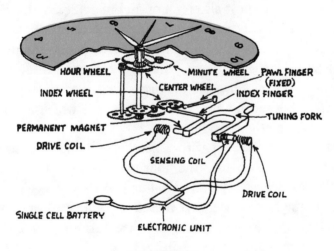

TUNING-FORK ELECTRONIC WATCH

HOUR WHEEL · MINUTE WHEEL · PAWL FINGER (FIXED) · INDEX WHEEL · CENTER WHEEL · INDEX FINGER · TUNING FORK · PERMANENT MAGNET · DRIVE COIL · SENSING COIL · DRIVE COIL · SINGLE CELL BATTERY · ELECTRONIC UNIT

FIGURE 131

The index finger is attached to one prong of the tuning fork, and its back-and-forth movement turns the index wheel. A train of gears cuts down the number of turns transferred by the index wheel until the center wheel is turning 24 times in 24 hours. The rest of the watch is like an electric watch.

CALENDAR WATCHES

Calendar watches not only tell time in seconds, minutes, and hours, but also tell the day of the week and the date (day of the month). Some watches also tell the month. The days, weeks, and months are seen through small windows in the face of the watch (Fig. 132).

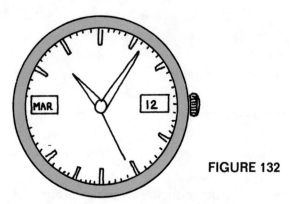

FIGURE 132

A *simple* calendar watch changes the day of the week and the date every 24 hours and the month every 31 days. At the end of each 30-day month, you must reset the watch by hand to skip the 31st day that appears on other months. You must also reset on February 28 and on February 29 of leap years. A *perpetual* calendar watch never needs resetting.

The names of the months and days of the week and the numbers that show the date are etched into, or printed upon, small discs, segments of which appear in the windows. These discs are turned by a gear train that is separate from the second-minute-hour train, but which is driven by the same mainspring or other energy source.

The calendar train begins with a gear wheel—the *hour wheel*—which fits around the arbor that turns the hour hand. This gear wheel turns two *intermediate gear wheels* (Fig. 133). Each of these wheels has twice as many teeth as the hour wheel and therefore each turns once as the hour wheel turns twice. So, each intermediate wheel turns once in 24 hours.

On the rim of each intermediate gear wheel is a *pin*. Once during each revolution of an intermediate gear wheel, a pin strikes a tooth of a gear that has triangular teeth and is called a *star wheel*. The star wheels turn arbors, to which are attached the discs that carry the days of the week and the date numbers. The *weekday star wheel* has 7 teeth and the *date star wheel* has 31 teeth. The pin pushes aside one tooth of a star wheel and then moves on. The action of the pin on one intermediate wheel causes the weekday star wheel to make ⅐ of a turn. On the side of the star wheel opposite the pin is a *jumper spring*. Attached to one end of this spring is a triangular piece of metal that fits between two teeth of the

168

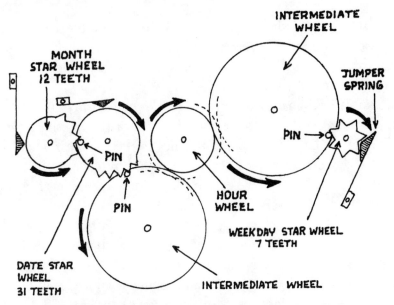

star wheel and holds the wheel in position. As the pin begins to move the star wheel, a new tooth pushes against the triangular piece, bending the spring outward. Immediately after the point of the star wheel passes the apex of the triangular piece, the tension of the spring pulls the star wheel into a new position and holds it. The sudden movement of the star wheel jumps a new day into place beneath the window in the face of the watch. The action of the jumper spring makes sure that the star wheel advances precisely ⅟₇ of a turn, and therefore the proper day is positioned exactly within the window.

The date is advanced in the same manner as the day, but the date star wheel, having 31 teeth, makes only ⅟₃₁ of a turn at midnight. The *month star wheel*, which has 12 teeth, is turned by a pin on the date star wheel. Since the date star wheel completes one turn in a month, the month star wheel is given ⅟₁₂ of a turn at the end of each month.

Figure 134-A shows the gear train of a perpetual calendar watch. Although the wheels are shown as circles for the sake of simplicity, they actually are toothed wheels, or gears.

A *lever* rocks back and forth, turning around a pivot. At one end of the lever is a *heel* and a *toe*. The other end is tapered, forming the *tail*. A lightly tensioned spring, located at the pivot, holds the lever in such a position that a cam on the 24-hour intermediate wheel can make contact with the heel once every 24 hours.

Screwed to the date star wheel is a flat plate called a *snail* (because it is shaped like a snail shell). Just behind the toe of the lever is a click which pivots on a small screw. The free end of the click is held upon the edge of the snail by another lightly tensioned spring. As the snail turns, the free end of the click moves around its edge.

The tail is held against the rim of the *four-year wheel* by pressure of the same spring that holds the heel in the path of the intermediate wheel cam. The tip of the tail drops into notches in the four-year wheel as that wheel turns. This makes the lever sensitive to any changes in the shape of the edge of the four-year wheel, so the attitude of the lever changes as the four-year wheel turns.

Figure 134-B is a much exaggerated drawing of a four-year wheel. The segment of a wheel above and to the right shows the notches in proper proportion. During a 31-day month, the tail rides on the edge of the wheel. During a 30-day month, the tail drops into and rides in one of the shallow notches cut in the wheel. In a leap-year February (29 days long), the tail is in a slightly deeper notch, and during the other three Februarys (28 days each) in four years, the tail is in one of the three deepest notches.

During any 31-day month, while the tail of the lever is slowly moving along the edge of the four-year wheel, the 24-hour intermediate wheel completes 31 revolutions; with each revolution, the cam pushes the lever over and causes the toe to engage the 31-toothed date star wheel, moving it forward one notch. At the end of the month, the date star wheel will have completed one revolution.

We have seen that screwed to the date star wheel is a snail upon which the click rides. As the snail turns, the step in the snail approaches the click until, on the day before the last day of a month (when the toe of the lever moves across to engage the date star wheel), the click engages the step in the snail. Then both the toe and click advance the date star wheel by one tooth.

Also, during the 31-day month, the date star wheel has been advancing the four-year-wheel drive wheel by one tooth each day until, at the end of the month, an index pin on the four-year-wheel drive wheel advances the four-year wheel by one tooth, the equivalent of one month. While the four-year wheel is being advanced, the cam of the 24-hour intermediate wheel is engaging the lever. This action holds the tail clear of the four-year wheel as that wheel advances. When the four-year wheel has completed its forward movement, the intermediate wheel cam releases the lever, allowing the tail to return to contact with the four-year wheel. If the completed 31-day month is followed by a 30-day month, the tail will be resting in one of the shallow notches.

170

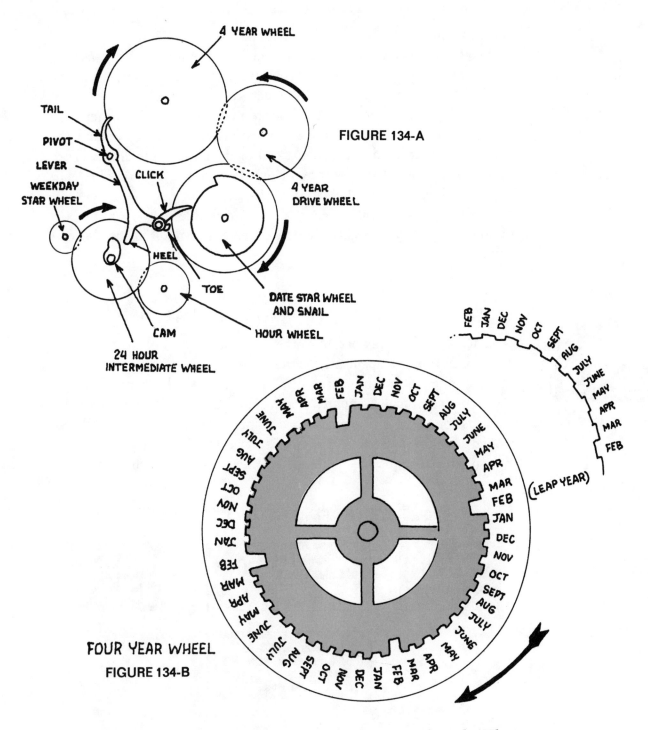

4 YEAR WHEEL

FIGURE 134-A

TAIL

PIVOT

LEVER

WEEKDAY
STAR WHEEL

CLICK

4 YEAR
DRIVE WHEEL

HEEL

TOE

DATE STAR WHEEL
AND SNAIL

CAM

HOUR WHEEL

24 HOUR
INTERMEDIATE WHEEL

(LEAP YEAR)

FOUR YEAR WHEEL
FIGURE 134-B

In its new position, the tail is leaning slightly farther to the right. This causes the lower end of the lever to move to the left and take the toe slightly farther from the date star wheel. The click then slides a short distance around the edge of the snail and begins its month-long journey slightly forward of where it had rested at the beginning of a 31-day month. The previous cycle is now completed in 30 days. At the end of this period, the click engages the step in the snail and advances the date star wheel by two teeth. When the lever is released from the influence of the cam, the four-year wheel will have been advanced by another tooth, and the tail will again be in contact with the edge of that wheel.

The deeper notches cause the lever to move the toe still farther from the date star wheel and cause the click to begin its journey around the snail still farther in advance. At the end of its journey, the click will advance the date star wheel by three or four teeth, depending on the depth of the notch in which the tail has been riding.

Because the perpetual calendar gear train is able to measure months of four different lengths, the watch never needs resetting at the end of any month.

FIGURE 135

DIGITAL, OR ILLUMINATED CRYSTAL, WATCH

This watch has only one moving part, a tiny crystal of quartz. There is no mainspring, escapement, electromagnets, gears, pinions, hands, nor calendar discs. Substituting for these parts is a small electric cell (or battery), a very small computer, and a liquid crystal. Time is shown by numbers composed of lozenge-shaped points of light against a dark background (Fig. 135). Between the numbers that tell the hours and minutes are two vertically positioned points of light that flash once each second.

CIRCUITS OF DIGITAL ELECTRONIC WATCH

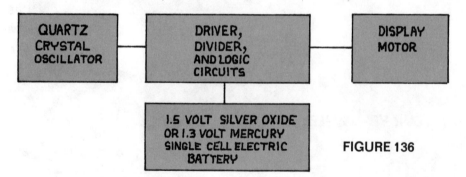

FIGURE 136

Figure 136 is a diagram that shows how the parts of a digital watch are arranged. The source of energy is either a 1.5-volt silver oxide, or a 1.3-volt mercury, electric cell.

The *quartz crystal oscillator* contains a very small sliver of quartz that is connected to the electric cell. When alternating current of proper frequency is sent into the quartz crystal, it oscillates, or moves back and forth, very rapidly. It does this 32,768 times per second. The frequency of the current is regulated and sent into the crystal by the *driver circuit*. This circuit, plus the logic circuits, contain about 900 extremely small transistors.

The *divider circuit*, which contains about 400 transistors, divides the oscillations of the quartz crystal by slightly more than 5,460, in a number of steps. The result is a series of electrical impulses one second apart. The purpose of starting with so large a number of oscillations and then stepping them down is accuracy. Dividing a very large number allows you to miss by a few units and still retain high accuracy. A digital watch is set to an accuracy of ½ part per 1,000,000, which is equivalent to 1½ seconds per year. However, aging and variations in temperature lower this accuracy to about 10 seconds per month, or 2 minutes per year.

The *logic* is the computer unit, which is programmed to use the timed electrical impulses to regulate the *display motor*. This is not a motor in the usual sense of being a machine that runs in the manner of an automobile motor or an electric motor. It is a device that causes the display of lighted numbers to work. It is made up of a number of diodes, each of which may be thought of as half a transistor. The diodes used in a digital watch give off light energy when electric current enters them. The diodes for displaying each number or letter are grouped in a matrix of rows and columns. The logic circuit switches current to the proper combination of diodes that will form the numbers needed to tell the time at any moment.

Light energy produced by the diodes is projected into a *liquid crystal*, a colorless substance called a *phospholipid*. When light energy enters this substance, it turns color or glows. The phospholipid used in a digital watch is contained in a plastic case shaped so as to magnify the points of light produced by entering light energy. As the energy from the changing combinations of energy-emitting diodes enters the liquid crystal, numbers glow brightly on the face of the watch.

CLOCKS

In the modern world, where most people tell time by watches and check the accuracy of their watches by radio time signals, clocks have two principal uses: (1) as ornamental pieces of furniture, since many clocks are beautiful; and (2) in public places, such as classrooms and factories, where large numbers of people all have a need to agree on the time.

SPRING-DRIVEN CLOCK

Some clocks are simply large watches. They derive their energy from a mainspring and have gear trains and escapements, as a watch does. The mainspring is wound by a key which fits into the back of the clock's case or into a hole in the face.

PENDULUM CLOCK

A pendulum clock has no mainspring. Energy for turning the wheels and for the escapement comes from the pull of a weight. Since weight is due to the force of gravity, a clock works on gravitational energy.

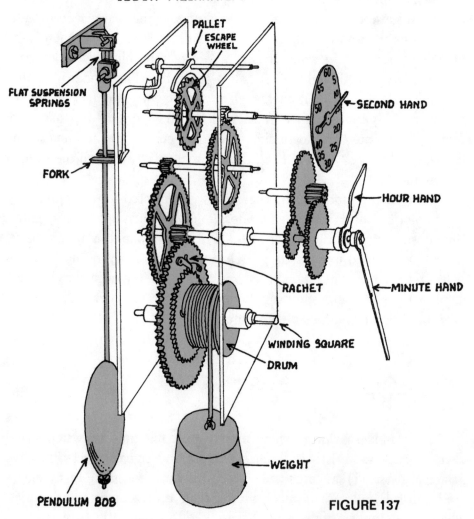

CLOCK MECHANISM

PALLET
ESCAPE WHEEL
FLAT SUSPENSION SPRINGS
SECOND HAND
FORK
HOUR HAND
RACHET
MINUTE HAND
WINDING SQUARE
DRUM
PENDULUM BOB
WEIGHT

FIGURE 137

174

The weight is attached to a long chain which is attached to a drum (Fig. 137). To wind the chain upon the drum, you turn the drum by means of a key that fits into the back of the clock. The key actually turns a gear that turns a winding wheel, and the winding wheel turns the drum. This is somewhat like the way the barrel of a watch is turned by the crown and stem. The chain is kept from being immediately unwound, because the drum is attached to a ratchet wheel. The chain unwinds the drum slowly as the drum is allowed to revolve through the turning of a gear train and escapement. Clocks use two main kinds of escapements (Fig. 138).

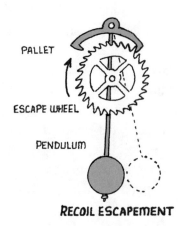

RECOIL ESCAPEMENT

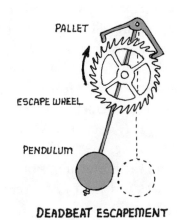

DEADBEAT ESCAPEMENT

Escapement gives pendulum a push before it reaches the center of its swing (dotted figure). Pendulum continuing past center causes escape wheel to recoil.

Escapement gives pendulum a push at the center of its swing (dotted figure). Pallets fit flat against teeth of escape wheel which cannot recoil. This escapement is more accurate.

FIGURE 138

You will remember that in the escapement of a watch, the around-and-back swing of the balance wheel governs the timing of the escape wheel movements. In a pendulum clock, the escapement is timed by the pendulum. A clock pendulum is a metal rod that has a weight at one end. The weight is called a *bob*. The time it takes a pendulum to travel from the highest point at one end of its swing to the highest point at the other end is the *period* of the pendulum.

The period of a pendulum varies with the length of the pendulum, but not with the weight of the bob. More precisely, the period varies according to the distance between the top of the rod and the center of the bob. A short pendulum has a shorter period than a long pendulum. To say these things mathematically, the period of a pendulum varies according to the square root of the length of the rod. This means that if you increase the length of the rod by four, you cut the length of its period in half. But if you increase the weight of the pendulum bob by four—or any other amount—you do not change the period at all.

As in a watch, the escapement governs how accurately the clock keeps time. The rate at which the escapement works depends on the period of the pendulum. And, as we learned, the length of the period depends on the length of the rod. The pendulum rod expands and becomes longer when the temperature rises. The rod contracts, becoming shorter, when the temperature falls. This means that in warm weather a pendulum clock runs more slowly than in cool weather. To correct for changes in temperature, you could move the bob up the rod in warm weather and down in cool weather. This adjustment actually was made on clocks at one time. It was an improvement on clocks without movable pendulum bobs, but it was not very accurate. Modern pendulum clocks have *compensating pendulums* (Fig. 139). When the temperature rises and the rod lengthens downward, the two columns of mercury in the bob lengthen upward. The two changes in length offset each other and the pendulum period does not change.

As a pendulum swings, it loses energy because it is slowed by the pull of gravity, by the friction of the air upon the rod and bob, and by the elastic action of the suspension spring from which the pendulum hangs. The pendulum overcomes the forces that act to slow it and is kept swinging by being given a small push as it passes the lowest point of each swing. The push comes from the fork which is continually transferring energy from the weight to the pendulum through a gear train and the

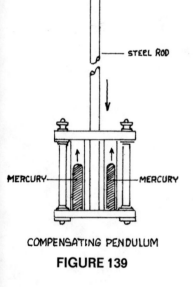

COMPENSATING PENDULUM

FIGURE 139

POINT OF SUPPORT

STEEL ROD

MERCURY

MERCURY

FIGURE 140

176

escapement. The fork needs to give the pendulum only a very small push to make up for the loss of energy. It is similar to what you do when you push someone sitting on a swing. After you start the swing, you need only a small push at some point in each period to keep the swing going (Fig. 140).

There are electrically driven pendulum clocks. These do not have weights or chains. Instead, the swings of the pendulum open and close the contacts of an electric switch. Each time the contacts close, an electromagnet gives the pendulum a push.

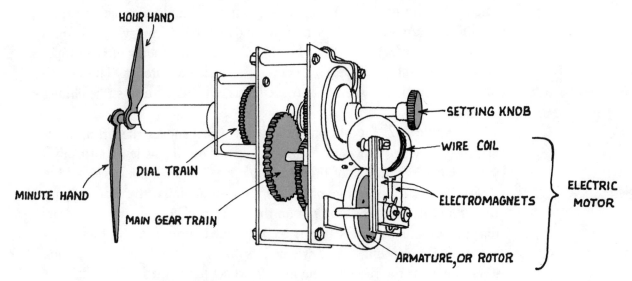

HOUR HAND

SETTING KNOB

WIRE COIL

DIAL TRAIN

MINUTE HAND

ELECTROMAGNETS

ELECTRIC MOTOR

MAIN GEAR TRAIN

ARMATURE, OR ROTOR

MOVEMENT OF AN ELECTRIC CLOCK

FIGURE 141

ELECTRIC CLOCKS

Energy to turn the wheels of an electric clock does not come from within the clock, but from a generator at an electric generating plant. A wire attached to the clock is plugged into a wall outlet and the clock receives electric current through wires in the same manner as other household appliances do. The current is *alternating current* (AC). It changes the direction in which it flows 60 times each second. The current turns a *synchronous motor* (Fig. 141). The speed at which this kind of motor turns is governed by the number of electrical pulses sent through the wires by the electric generator. This number, 120 each second—60 in one direction and 60 in the other—is carefully controlled at the generating station, so that the number of pulses varies very little over long periods. Therefore, an electric clock rarely gains or loses time.

There are clocks that not only show the time on their faces, but tell time by playing chimes or striking chimes or bells at regular intervals. Alarm clocks ring a bell at any time that you choose.

Chiming and alarm clocks have a separate source of energy for working the chimes or alarm bells. This source may be a hand-wound spring, a set of weights, or an electric motor.

Although the arrangement of gears and other devices that produce the chimes and alarms are quite complicated—commonly more complicated than the time-measuring arrangement—all kinds have some things in common. As in a clock, a ratchet holds back the energy source from giving up its energy in a single burst. To release the energy at the proper time, one or more pins push aside and unlock the ratchet. The energy source can then turn gears that move levers, which, in turn, strike chimes or bells.

In Figure 142, the pin on the minute wheel moves the *lifting lever* upward, carrying with it the *warning lever*. The lifting lever also raises the *rack hook* by means of the *rack hook pin*. The rack hook releases the *rack*. The rack drops to one of the steps on the *snail*. At the same instant, the *stop lever* clears the *stop pin* on the *locking wheel*. The train of gears that moves striking levers begins to turn, but is immediately stopped by a pin on the *warning wheel* which hits the *stop piece* on the warning lever. Then, at the moment the minute wheel has turned to the time the clock is to chime or strike, the pin passes the lifting lever. This allows the warning lever to drop. The warning wheel is now freed and the chiming or striking begins.

Note that the distance from the center of the snail to the edge of a step—its radius—increases as the step is located farther around the snail in a clockwise direction. Due to the increase in radius, the distance that the rack can drop is different for each step it strikes. It drops farthest when it strikes the step with the shortest radius. Note also that, as the radius of the steps increases, so does the length of their edges.

The turning of the snail raises the rack, and the rack hook slides down each tooth until it drops off the last one. The *stop lever*, which is attached to the rack hook, falls and contacts the *stop pin* in the locking wheel. This stops the chiming or striking action.

The shortest step allows the clock time enough to strike or chime only once (for 1 o'clock) and the longest allows the chiming or striking to work 12 times (for 12 o'clock).

If a clock is to chime at each quarter hour, additional gear wheels are

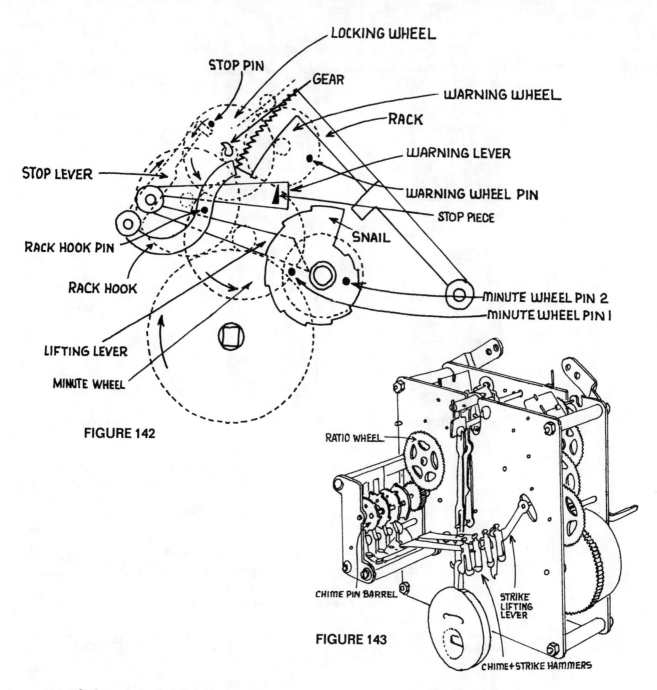

LOCKING WHEEL

STOP PIN

GEAR

WARNING WHEEL

RACK

WARNING LEVER

STOP LEVER

WARNING WHEEL PIN

STOP PIECE

SNAIL

RACK HOOK PIN

MINUTE WHEEL PIN 2

MINUTE WHEEL PIN 1

RACK HOOK

LIFTING LEVER

MINUTE WHEEL

FIGURE 142

RATIO WHEEL

CHIME PIN BARREL

STRIKE LIFTING LEVER

FIGURE 143

CHIME+STRIKE HAMMERS

provided so that the foregoing chiming action may take place four times an hour.

Figure 143 shows one kind of chime movement. The chime and strike hammers hit four metal rods (not shown in the illustration) which are of different lengths, each giving forth a different note. The *chime pin barrel* controls the levers that move the hammers. The four discs that make up the barrel each have four teeth at different locations on their rims. As the discs turn, the teeth contact and lift the levers. As a tooth passes the contact, the lever falls and the hammer strikes a chime rod. Different locations of the teeth produce different tunes in different clocks. A well-known quarter-hour chime is shown in Fig. 144.

179

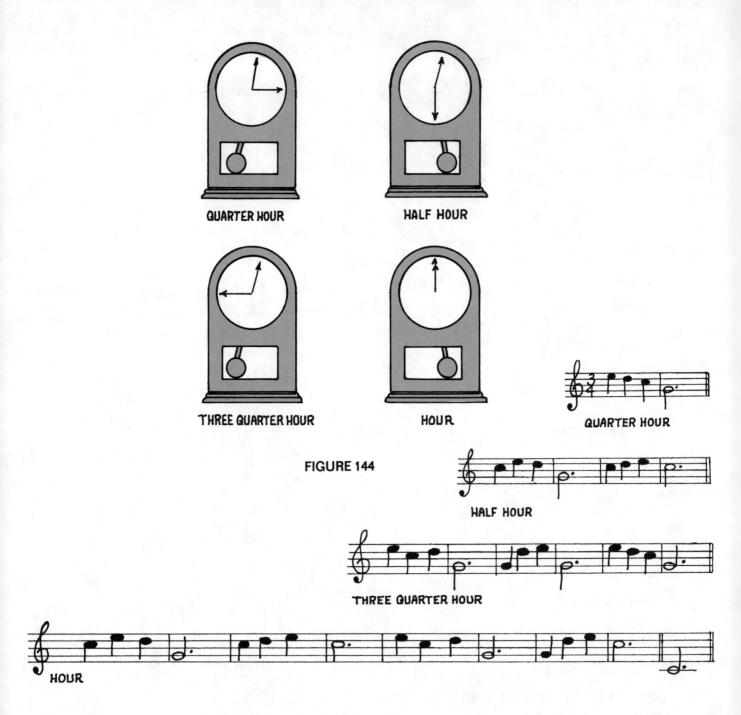

QUARTER HOUR

HALF HOUR

THREE QUARTER HOUR

HOUR

FIGURE 144

QUARTER HOUR

HALF HOUR

THREE QUARTER HOUR

HOUR

THE ATOMIC CLOCK

Scientists have discovered how to count the vibrations—the rapid back-and-forth movements—of atoms that make up certain elements. An atom then becomes a kind of extremely small pendulum. Such a pendulum moves back and forth billions of times per second. By measuring the rate of vibration precisely, scientists have been able to use the vibrating atoms as clocks that are accurate to one part in 100 trillion. This means that an atomic clock will not gain or lose even one second in 3,420,000 years!

180

OPTICAL INSTRUMENTS

Optical instruments—mirrors, magnifying glasses, eyeglasses, microscopes, telescopes, and others—help you see things better than you can see them with your unaided eyes.

All optical instruments make use of mirrors, lenses, or prisms as parts of the instrument. These are devices for controlling light. Before we can understand how optical instruments work, we must know a little about light and what it does when it is reflected or passes through transparent materials.

REFLECTION

Physicists accept two explanations of the nature of light (Fig. 145). One describes light as streams of extremely small particles which travel in straight lines in all directions from a luminous source such as a candle flame, a light bulb, or the sun. The other explanation describes light as bundles of waves. The waves travel outward from a luminous source in much the same way as water waves move outward from the place where a stone falls into water. The second explanation is the one generally used by scientists when they describe how optical instruments work. A bundle of light waves all traveling in the same direction from the same source is a *light ray*.

LIGHT AS PARTICLES

LIGHT AS WAVES

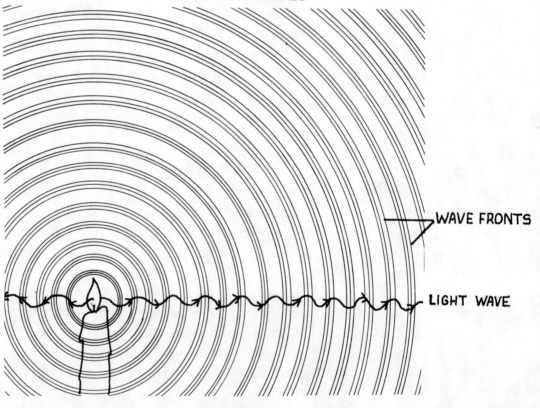

WAVE FRONTS

LIGHT WAVE

182   **FIGURE 145**

When light strikes an object, some light rays bounce off the object (Fig. 146). This light is *reflected*. Smooth surfaces reflect light best. Rough surfaces scatter many of the light waves, reflecting only a small number. Light waves are reflected at an angle that is the same as the one at which they arrive. You can illustrate this by throwing a ball at a wall. If you throw the ball straight at the wall, the angle of its path is zero, so it bounces straight back at you at a zero angle. If the ball strikes the wall at a 45° angle, it will rebound at a 45° angle, and so on, for any angle.

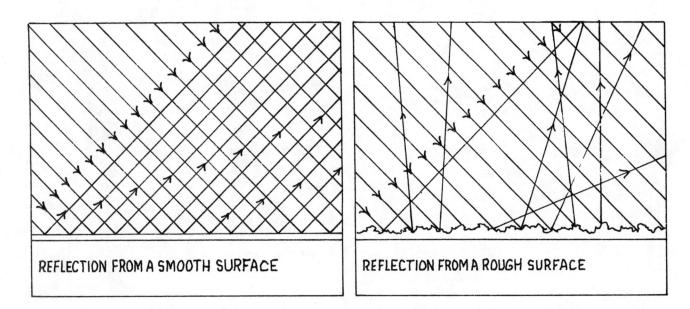

REFLECTION FROM A SMOOTH SURFACE   REFLECTION FROM A ROUGH SURFACE

FIGURE 146

FLAT MIRROR

The simplest optical instrument is a flat, or plane, mirror. It consists of a flat piece of metal polished very smooth or a thin coating of silver or some other silvery-white metal deposited chemically on one surface of a flat sheet of glass. The glass simply provides a support for the very thin shiny coating.

When you are in front of a mirror, you see an image of yourself "in the mirror." You appear to be behind the mirror, although the light rays that enter your eyes are reflected from the surface of the mirror and not from a distance behind it (Fig. 147). Your reflection in the mirror is called a *virtual image*, because the image only seems to be where you see it; it does not actually exist there.

183

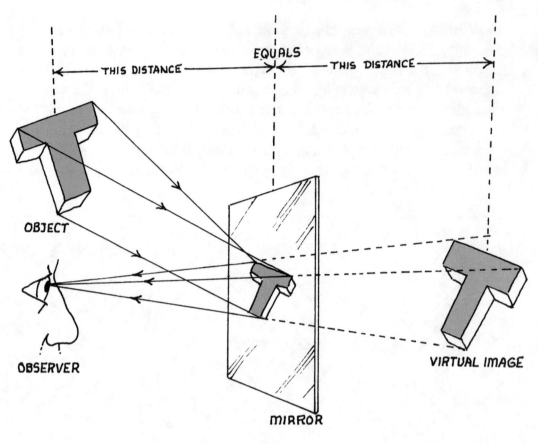

OBJECT

OBSERVER

MIRROR

VIRTUAL IMAGE

FIGURE 147

A virtual image in a plane mirror (1) is the same size as the reflected object; (2) seems to be at the same distance behind the mirror as the object is in front of the mirror; and (3) is reversed along a line running straight through, or perpendicular to, the surface of the mirror.

Let us take a moment to understand the last of these statements. Most people believe that a mirror turns images around from right to left or vice versa. This belief comes from the fact that if you hold an object such as a book up to a mirror, the print is reversed from right to left— "it reads backward." However, think for a moment what you do when you "hold a book up to a mirror." You turn the book around, so that the printing which ordinarily reads from your left to your right, now runs from right to left. And the mirror reflects the turned-around printing. But the mirror did not turn the printing around, *you* did. A simple way to prove that a mirror does not reverse images from side to side is to write a word on a pane of glass with a grease pencil or a lipstick. Then hold the pane in front of a mirror, *without turning it around*. The letters you see in the mirror will not be reversed; they will read from left to right, as you

184

printed them. Then turn the pane around as you would a book held before a mirror. The letters of the word now are turned around.

Although a mirror does not reverse images from side to side, it does reverse them from front to back, or along a line perpendicular to the surface of the mirror (Fig. 147). If you face north and look into a mirror directly in front of you, your virtual image will be facing south. If you are a foot—or any other distance—in front of the mirror, your image will seem to be the same distance behind the mirror. Thus, the mirror seems to turn you around.

Although a plane mirror does not reverse images from left to right, or vice versa, there is a sense in which it seems to do so. If you look into a mirror and touch your right ear, you will see that a hand on the right side of your mirror image touches an ear on the right side of the mirror image (Fig. 148). You would expect this, since you know that the mirror does not reverse sides. But the mirror has reversed your image from front to back. So, if you were facing in the same direction as your image, you would *consider* the hand in the mirror to be your left hand touching your left ear. This is something you would be thinking into the reflection. It is not due to anything that happens because of the way reflected light acts.

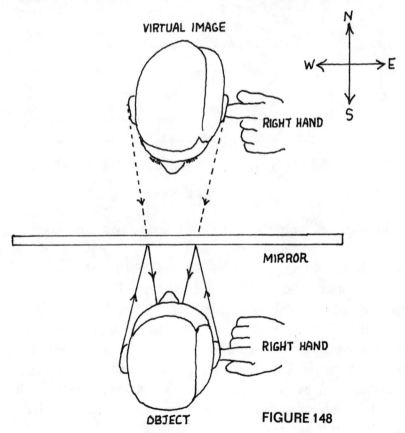

FIGURE 148

CURVED MIRROR

Many optical instruments use curved mirrors. Reflections from curved mirrors are quite different from those in plane mirrors. The mirror shown in Figure 149 is curved through one-quarter of a circle. And light is reflected from its inwardly curved surface. It is a *concave* mirror. (Actually, the mirror is one-quarter of a sphere, not a circle, but the diagram shows a cross section cut through the sphere.) The straight lines represent light rays. The dot CC is at the *center of curvature*. This is the center of the sphere of which the mirror is one quarter. Light rays reflected by the mirror meet at a point marked F. This is the *principal focus*.

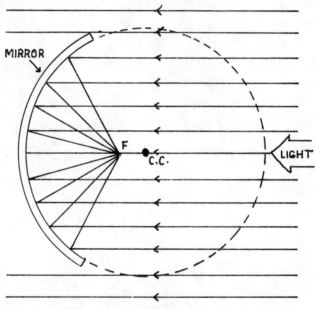

F = PRINCIPAL FOCUS   CC = CENTER OF CURVATURE

FIGURE 149

In a curved mirror, the kind of image you see—whether larger or smaller than the object, whether right-side-up or upside down—depends on where the reflected object is located. Figures 150-A to 150-F show images of objects (arrows) at three locations. Dotted lines mean that the image is virtual; solid lines mean that it is *real*. A real image exists in space. If you hold a white card where the image is, it will be projected upon the card like a movie upon a screen. Concave mirrors are used in optical instruments to concentrate light into beams of various shapes.

A mirror that is outwardly curved is *convex*. No matter what the distance of an object from a convex mirror, the image is always virtual, behind the mirror, right-side-up, and smaller.

186

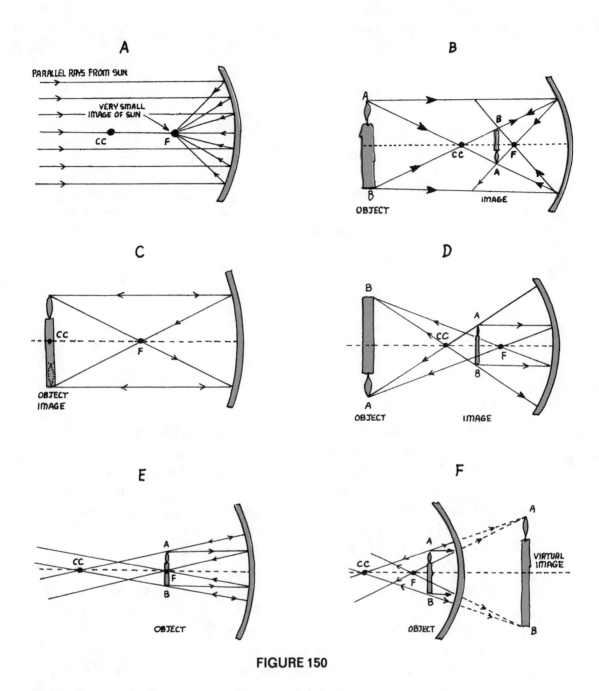

FIGURE 150

REFRACTION

Light passes through a *transparent* substance so well that you can see objects on the other side clearly. Light rays entering a transparent substance, such as glass, water, or diamond, are bent, or *refracted*, as if they enter at less than a 90° angle. Figure 151 shows light rays passing through a piece of window glass.

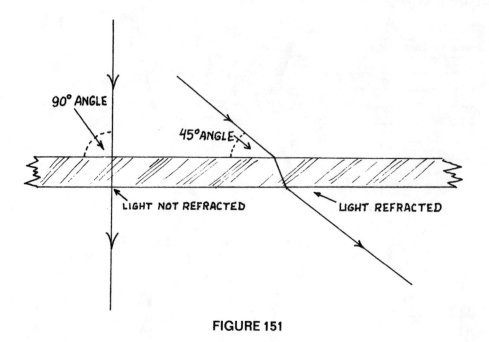

FIGURE 151

To understand why refraction takes place, imagine a column of soldiers marching diagonally off a paved road into a field of sand (Fig. 152). The sand will slow each soldier as he steps into it. In each rank the first soldiers to enter the sand will be those at your left (the soldiers' right). As these soldiers are slowed, the ones to the right continue their faster pace until they, too, are slowed by entering the sand. Each rank will bend to the left until all the soldiers in that rank have entered the sand. Eventually, the whole column is bent to the left. And with all the soldiers slowed equally by the sand, the rank will automatically straighten.

In place of the soldiers, think of a ray of light—a bundle of light waves. As the waves enter the glass, they are slowed and they are bent, or refracted. Light waves are bent only when they enter a transparent substance at an angle that is less than a right angle, or 90° angle (Fig. 151). You can understand why this is true if you think of the soldiers marching straight into the sand, that is, at a right angle to the edge of the road. The sand would slow all the soldiers in each rank equally, so no swinging around of any ranks or bending of the whole column would take place.

When the light ray that entered the glass at a less-than-90° angle leaves the glass, it is bent again, this time in the opposite direction. As the light leaves the glass, it travels as fast as it did before entering. The increased speed causes the ray to bend in the opposite direction. Think of the soldiers marching out of the sand and upon another paved road

188

(Fig. 152). The opposite of what took place when they entered the sand now happens. The first soldiers in each rank march faster as they step upon the hard road. This causes each rank to swing to the right and the whole column bends to the right.

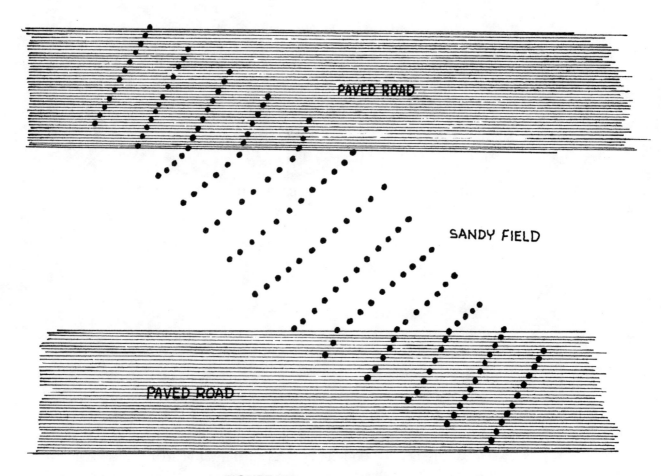

FIGURE 152

PRISM

A prism is a piece of glass or other transparent substance that has at least two flat sides. If a light ray in a prism is refracted at an angle greater than a certain amount, the ray cannot leave the prism. Instead, it is re-flected from a surface of the prism. So, prisms can be used both in refracting and reflecting light. Figure 153 shows a number of prisms, and how they refract and reflect light.

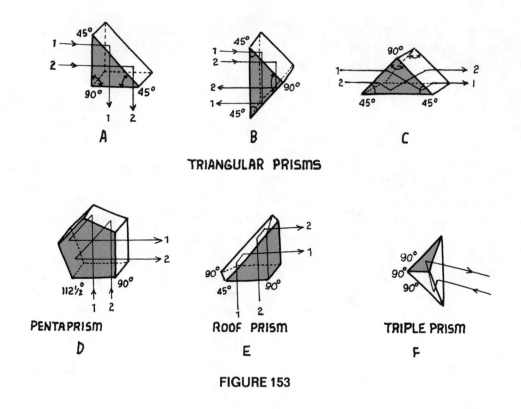

TRIANGULAR PRISMS

PENTAPRISM
D

ROOF PRISM
E

TRIPLE PRISM
F

FIGURE 153

LENS

Suppose we put two triangular prisms together, base to base. Figure 154 shows how light rays would be refracted through them. Now, suppose we grind the edges off each prism, making a smoothly curved solid. And finally, suppose we grind a single piece of glass into the shape of two curved prisms. We would have a *lens*. The kind of lens we would get by starting with the triangular prisms joined base to base is a *double-convex* lens, because both its surfaces are outward-curving. If we start with two triangular prisms joined apex to apex, we get a *double-concave* lens, with both surfaces curving inward.

A double-convex lens brings together light rays at point F, which is the *principal focus*. A double-concave lens refracts light rays by spreading them. As with mirrors, the size of the image depends on how far from the lens the object is. It also depends on how much the light rays are refracted. The more the rays are bent, the more the size of the image is increased or decreased. A thick lens with sharply curved surfaces bends light rays more than they are bent by a thin flat lens.

In optical instruments, mirrors are used to reflect light rays, lenses are used to bend light rays, and prisms are used to both reflect and bend light rays.

190

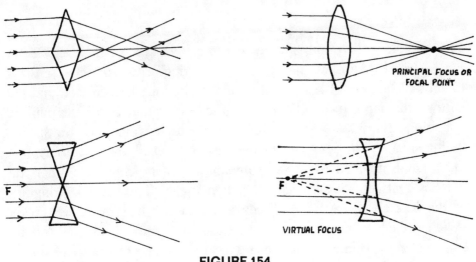

PRINCIPAL FOCUS OR FOCAL POINT

F

VIRTUAL FOCUS

FIGURE 154

EYEGLASSES

To understand how eyeglasses work, you must know how eyes work. Not only eyeglasses, but all other optical instruments are designed to accord with the way that eyes are formed and work.

A human eye is a hollow ball about one inch in diameter (Fig. 155). It is covered by a tough white coat, called the *sclera*, which protects it from blows or cuts that are not too severe. The front of the eye bulges slightly. This bulge is called the *cornea*. It is made up of transparent tissue and is filled with a clear jellylike liquid, the *aqueous humor*. At the back of the cornea is a circular tissue with a hole in it. This tissue is the *iris*,

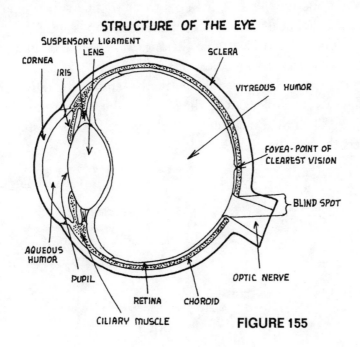

STRUCTURE OF THE EYE

SUSPENSORY LIGAMENT
LENS
CORNEA
IRIS
SCLERA
VITREOUS HUMOR
FOVEA - POINT OF CLEAREST VISION
BLIND SPOT
AQUEOUS HUMOR
PUPIL
OPTIC NERVE
RETINA
CHOROID
CILIARY MUSCLE
FIGURE 155

191

and the hole is the pupil. The iris is the colored part of the eye. On the inner edge of the iris, around the pupil, is a ring of tiny muscles, sensitive to light. When bright light strikes the eye, the muscles contract, and this narrows the pupil. In dim light, the muscles relax and widen the pupil.

Behind the iris is a circular double-convex lens made of transparent flexible tissue. The lens is attached to the eyeball by *suspensory ligaments*, and attached to these ligaments are *ciliary muscles*. When the muscles contract, the suspensory ligaments relax. The natural springiness of the lens tissue causes it to contract and the lens becomes thicker. When the ciliary muscles relax, the ligaments contract and pull on the lens, making it thinner. These changes in the shape of the lens vary the amount by which light is bent as it passes through the lens. The result is that the eye can focus both near and far objects on a point at the back of the eyeball.

The main cavity of the eye also is filled with a clear jellylike liquid, the *vitreous humor*. Light that has passed through the cornea, pupil, and lens now passes through the main cavity, going to the inner wall of the eye. Covering the inner wall is a lining made up of millions of cells that contain the endings of nerves. This lining is the *retina*. It rests on the *choroid coat*, a layer made up of a vast number of blood vessels. The cells of the retina are called *rods* and *cones* because of their shapes. We see very faint light and slight changes in amounts of light by means of the cones. With the rods we see bright light and colors. Great numbers of nerves from the rods and cones join at the lower part of the back of the eye. Here they form the *optic nerve* which goes to the brain. When light arrives at the retina, a chemical reaction takes place in the rods and cones and causes electrical impulses to move along the optic nerve. The brain interprets the impulses as the shapes and colors of the things we see.

Light entering the eye is focused by the lens on the retina (Fig. 156). Since the lens is double-convex, the image in the retina is upside down and backward. When the brain interprets the nerve impulses as images, it also interprets them as being right side up.

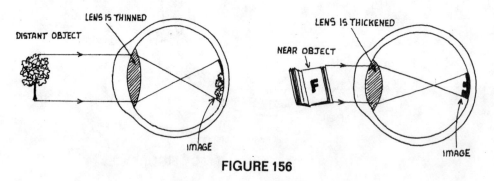

FIGURE 156

192

CORRECTIVE LENSES

The eyes of many people are not properly shaped. These people may have eyeballs that are too long or too short. They also may have poorly shaped lenses that are too thick or too thin.

If eyeballs are too long or lenses are too thick, the eye will be able to see nearby objects clearly, but far objects will be blurred. The owner of the eye will be *nearsighted*. When a person whose eyeballs are too long looks at far objects, his lens will not be able to become thin enough to focus light at a point on his retina. Instead, the light will be focused at a point in front of the retina (Fig. 157). The light rays cross at this focal

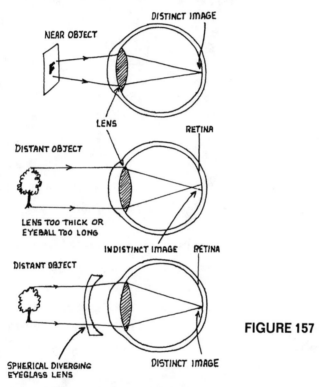

FIGURE 157

point, and when they reach the retina, they form a small circle instead of a sharp point of light. The result is a blurry image. The same thing happens if a person's lenses are too thick. A thick lens bends light rays more strongly than a thin lens does. As a result, light is focused in front of the retina. The lens is too thick to be pulled thin enough by the action of the muscles attached to it. Again, the light rays reach the retina as small circles instead of points, and the image they form is blurred.

A person whose eyeballs are too short or whose lenses are too thin will be able to see far objects clearly but close objects (such as letters in a book) will be blurs. This person is *farsighted*. His eyes reverse the situation of the nearsighted person. A short eyeball causes light from

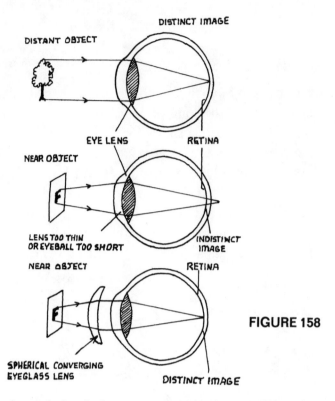

DISTANT OBJECT

DISTINCT IMAGE

EYE LENS RETINA

NEAR OBJECT

LENS TOO THIN
OR EYEBALL TOO SHORT

INDISTINCT
IMAGE

NEAR OBJECT RETINA

SPHERICAL CONVERGING
EYEGLASS LENS

DISTINCT IMAGE

FIGURE 158

close objects to focus behind the retina (Fig. 158). And so does a lens that is too thin.

We can correct the vision of a nearsighted or a farsighted eye by placing in front of it a lens that focuses light sharply on the retina. This is what the lenses of eyeglasses do.

In some eyes, the cornea is curved more from top to bottom than from side to side. In other eyes it is curved more from side to side. This defect is called *astigmatism*. Persons with astigmatism see things out of shape, something like the reflection in a curved mirror at an amusement park. Astigmatism can be corrected with eyeglass lenses that compensate for misshapen corneas. A lens for correcting side-to-side astigmatism is shown in Figure 159.

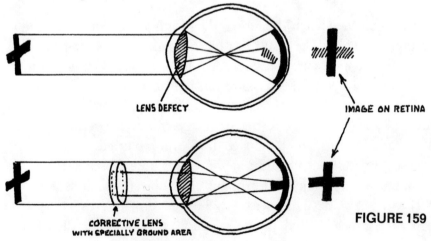

LENS DEFECT

IMAGE ON RETINA

CORRECTIVE LENS
WITH SPECIALLY GROUND AREA

FIGURE 159

194

BIFOCAL LENSES. The ability of an eye to focus on both near and distant objects is called *accommodation*. This ability is at its best when you are very young and it lessens as you grow older. When you pass the age of 40, your accommodation becomes difficult. Exactly what kind of problem a person will have when his accommodation becomes poor depends on what kind of eyesight he has had.

A person who has worn glasses to correct farsightedness will find that, when he loses accommodation, he cannot clearly see print in a book unless it is a few feet from his eyes. Even if he is able to hold the pages this far from his eyes, the distance makes the print too small to see. If he gets glasses for reading, he will not be able to wear them when he wants to see distant things.

A person who has had normal eyesight will have the same problem as a farsighted person, but not so severely. The person who had normal eyesight may be able to continue to get along without glasses, if he is willing to hold what he reads at arm's length.

A person who has worn glasses to correct nearsightedness will be able to see nearby small things if he takes off his glasses. But then he will not be able to see distant objects.

All these people can solve the problem of lessened accommodation by wearing *bifocal* lenses (Fig. 160). When grinding a bifocal lens, an optician shapes a small area so that it will focus nearby objects sharply on the retina. This area is at the bottom and on the side of the lens that will be worn nearest the nose. The rest of the lens is ground so that the eyeglass wearer can see distant objects.

A person wearing bifocals soon learns to look through the large upper parts of his eyeglass lenses when he wants to see distant things. He looks through the small area to see objects nearby. He does this automatically, without thinking about it.

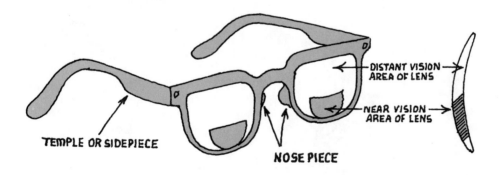

FIGURE 160

The frame into which eyeglass lenses are fitted does more than simply hold them on your face. A frame holds the lenses at the correct distance from your eyes, the correct height and side-to-side position, and the correct angle.

SIMPLE MICROSCOPE

A microscope is an optical instrument used for seeing small objects by producing enlarged images of them.

If you ever have seen pictures of the fictional detective, Sherlock Holmes, you probably saw him holding a *simple microscope,* or magnifying glass (Fig. 161). This is no more than a double-convex lens affixed in a metal frame attached to a handle. To use a magnifying glass, you move it nearer or farther from the object, until you see the object clearly —until the object is at the focus of the lens. The object will then be an enlarged virtual image. The number of times greater than natural size that a lens enlarges objects is called the *magnifying power* of the lens. A

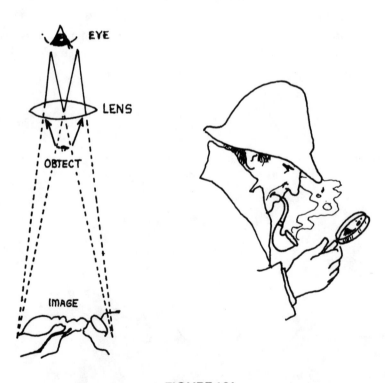

FIGURE 161

lens that magnifies 10 times is a 10-power lens. In writing, the letter "x" is used to stand for the words "times" or "power," as "10x."

Magnifying glasses are rarely made for enlarging images more than 20 times. The reason is that the larger an object is magnified, the more necessary it is to hold the magnifying glass steady in order to see a clear image. Most people cannot hold a magnifying glass steady enough if its power is more than 20.

COMPOUND MICROSCOPE

If you tried to make a magnifying glass with power greater than 20, you would find that the most powerful single lens you could make would magnify about 300 times. But you could easily magnify more than 300 times by using more than one lens. By placing one lens at the focus of another, the second lens magnifies the image produced by the first. You can see, then, that the magnifying power of a series of lenses is the product of all their powers. For example, if you use one lens of 10 power and one of 40 power, you can magnify 400 times (10x multiplied by 40x equals 400 power).

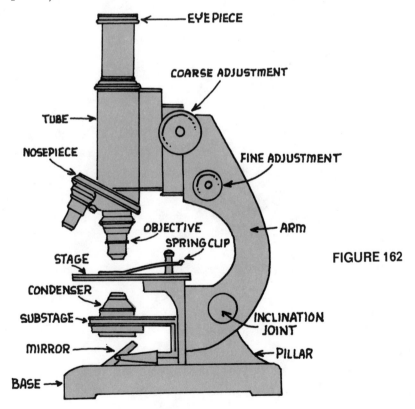

EYE PIECE

COARSE ADJUSTMENT

TUBE

NOSEPIECE

FINE ADJUSTMENT

OBJECTIVE

SPRING CLIP

ARM

STAGE

FIGURE 162

CONDENSER

SUBSTAGE

INCLINATION JOINT

MIRROR

PILLAR

BASE

A compound microscope has three main parts, the *base*, the *tube*, and the *body* (Fig. 162). The base is simply a heavy piece of metal in the shape of a two-pronged fork. It provides a steady base for the working parts of the microscope. The tube contains the lenses. The body supports the tube and contains mechanical devices for aiming and focusing the tube and for holding and lighting objects to be viewed.

The *coarse adjustment* and the *fine adjustment* are devices for raising and lowering the tube in order to focus the lenses. Both are knobs that turn gears, or pinions. The teeth of each pinion mesh with the teeth of a square metal bar. This arrangement is called a *rack and pinion*. The coarse adjustment rack and pinion has fewer and larger teeth. A small turn of the coarse adjustment knob moves the tube up or down a longer distance than the same turn of the fine adjustment.

The body includes the *stage*. This is a platform upon which you put the object you want to view. If the object is too thick for light to pass through, it must be lighted from above. But usually, the objects viewed with a microscope are thin and transparent or translucent. (A translucent object is one through which light can pass, but not well enough for you to see things through it clearly.) These objects are mounted on flat rectangles of glass called *slides* (Fig. 163). The slides are held firmly in place by two strips of springy metal called *spring clips*. Slides are lighted from below, so the stage has a hole in it.

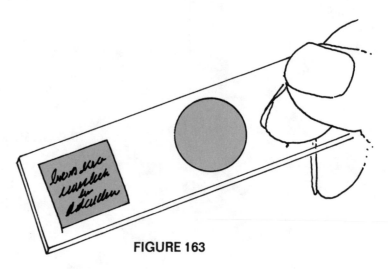

FIGURE 163

Light is directed upward by a mirror. The light passes from the mirror through a *condenser* that is attached to the *substage*. The condenser contains a lower lens, an *iris diaphragm*, and an upper lens. The iris diaphragm is made up of a number of thin metal blades, or *leaves*, hinged

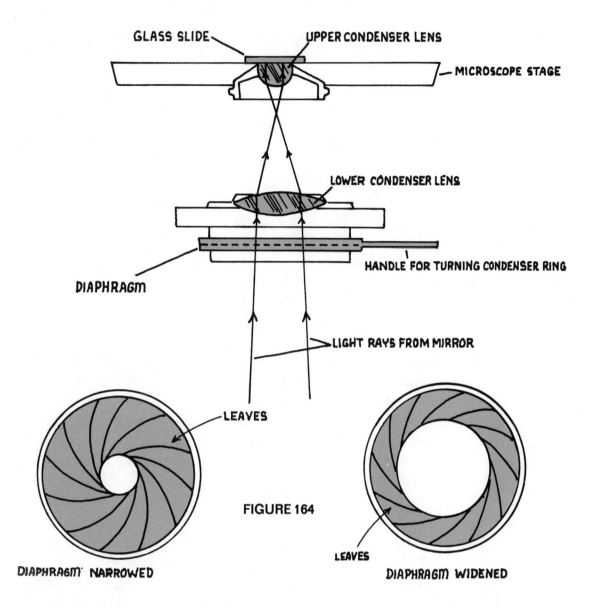

GLASS SLIDE

UPPER CONDENSER LENS

MICROSCOPE STAGE

LOWER CONDENSER LENS

HANDLE FOR TURNING CONDENSER RING

DIAPHRAGM

LIGHT RAYS FROM MIRROR

LEAVES

FIGURE 164

LEAVES

DIAPHRAGM NARROWED

DIAPHRAGM WIDENED

together so that they form a hole at their center (Fig. 164). They can move back and forth over each other. As they move, the hole becomes larger or smaller, depending on whether the blades are moving outward or inward. One end of each leaf is attached to the *condenser ring*. You can change the size of the hole by turning the ring. The purpose of the iris diaphragm is to increase or decrease the amount of light passing through the object on the slide. The iris diaphragm works much like the iris in your eye.

The most important part of a microscope is the tube. It is firmly supported by the solid metal arm on which is the rack-and-pinion. Within the tube are two groups of lenses. One group is at the top of the tube near where you place your eye when looking through the microscope. The other group is at the bottom, near the object you are viewing

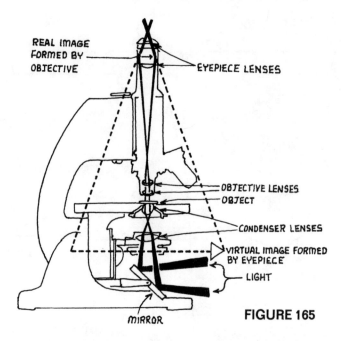

REAL IMAGE FORMED BY OBJECTIVE

EYEPIECE LENSES

OBJECTIVE LENSES

OBJECT

CONDENSER LENSES

VIRTUAL IMAGE FORMED BY EYEPIECE

LIGHT

MIRROR

FIGURE 165

(Fig. 165). The upper group is in a removable part of the tube called the *eyepiece*, or *ocular*. The power of the ocular lenses usually is 5x or 10x. The lower group of lenses is in a short tube called the *objective*. In modern microscopes, two to four objectives are attached to a revolving disc called the *nosepiece*. When you have decided which objective you want to use, you can move it into place at the lower end of the tube by turning the nosepiece. The objective lenses form a real and magnified image within the tube. The eyepiece lenses then magnify this real image, forming an enlarged virtual image.

Objectives contain from two to ten lenses. A frequently used set of objectives have powers of 3.5x, 10x, and 40x. A microscope using these objectives in combination with a 5x ocular would have magnifying powers of 17.5x, 50x, and 200x. A 10x ocular is frequently used. It increases the power of the microscope to 35x, 100x, and 400x. Some microscopes have a 97x objective, which is called an *oil immersion lens*. To use it, you put a drop of cedarwood oil on the slide and lower the tip of the objective lens into the oil. The oil intensifies the light that enters the objective.

The most powerful microscopes have 25x oculars and 100x objectives, giving a magnifying power of 2500x. With this combination of lenses, you can see objects that are a little less than 1/100,000 of an inch across.

Peering straight down into the eyepiece of a microscope that is in a vertical position can be inconvenient and uncomfortable. To overcome this problem, microscopes can be tilted backward to a comfortable viewing position. They have an *inclination joint* just above the base. It consists of a smooth bolt that runs through the lower part of the arm. It also passes through the *pillar*, which is part of the base. The bolt fits the hole very snugly. This causes the arm to turn stiffly, so that it will remain at the position to which you tilt it, and not move backward or forward due to its weight. Some microscopes have tubes bent at an angle, so that they do not need to be tilted. There is a prism in the tube to bend the light from the tube to the eyepiece.

A microscope that has one ocular may be tiring and a bit difficult to use. In order to keep from becoming tired by holding one eye shut, you view by keeping both eyes open. Although it is not at all hard to concentrate on what you see through the microscope, still, what you see with the other eye can be distracting. Also, what you see does not have the depth that comes from seeing objects with both eyes—stereo vision. To get around these difficulties, some microscopes have two eyepieces (Fig. 166), so that you can use both eyes at the same time and have stereo vision.

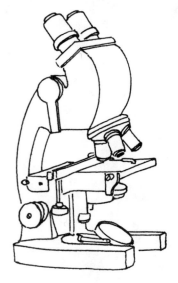

FIGURE 166

TELESCOPE

A telescope is an optical instrument for magnifying distant objects to make them appear closer. The system of lenses in a telescope is much like that of a microscope. An objective lens and an eyepiece lens (or sets of these two kinds of lenses) are contained within a tube. The two lenses work like those of a microscope: The objective lens produces a real image within the tube at the focal point of the eyepiece lens. The latter magnifies the image, forming an enlarged virtual image that seems to be directly in front of the telescope (Fig. 167).

Light arrives at a telescope from distant sources, such as a mountain peak, a star, or the moon. You cannot increase or decrease the amount of light entering the telescope as you can control the light that enters a microscope. Therefore, one of the goals in making a telescope is to bring to the eye as much light as possible.

Less light arrives at a telescope from a far object than from a near one. Let us see why. As light moves away from a source, the light rays diverge, or move farther apart. This is illustrated by the widening beam of light in Figure 168. A and B are two objective lenses of equal size. Lens B is twice as far as lens A from the source of light. All the light of the beam passes through lens A, but when the light reaches lens B, the beam has widened so much that half of it passes outside the lens. The illustration shows that only half as many light rays pass through lens B as through lens A. However, the diagram is a cross section, and if you were to make a calculation, you would find that only one-fourth as much light

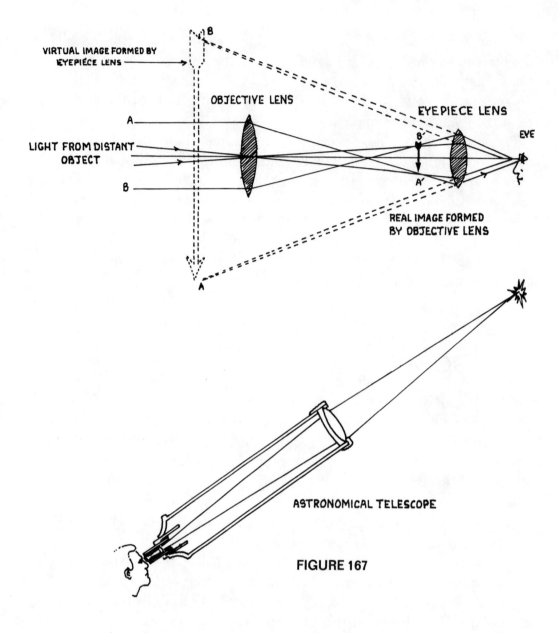

VIRTUAL IMAGE FORMED BY EYEPIECE LENS

OBJECTIVE LENS

EYEPIECE LENS

EYE

LIGHT FROM DISTANT OBJECT

REAL IMAGE FORMED BY OBJECTIVE LENS

ASTRONOMICAL TELESCOPE

FIGURE 167

passes through B as through A. For objective lens B to receive as much light as A, lens B would have to be twice as wide as A (as shown by the broken lines).

Since less light arrives at a telescope from a distant object, the objective lens of a telescope must be wide so as to admit as much light as possible. This explains why a telescope has an objective that is wider than its eyepiece—the opposite of a microscope.

There are two main ways of routing light through a telescope. The light may be directed entirely by refraction through the lenses. Telescopes that do this are *refractors*. Light also may be directed by reflection from mirrors. Telescopes that use mirrors are *reflectors*.

202

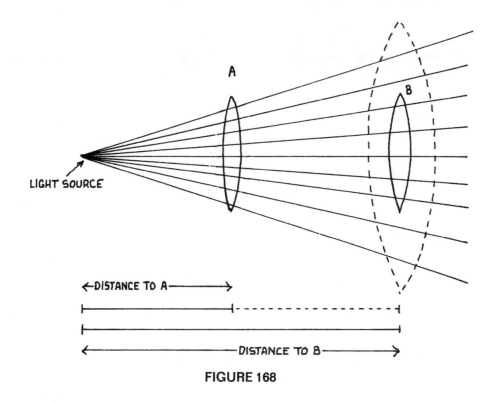

A

B

LIGHT SOURCE

←DISTANCE TO A——→

DISTANCE TO B

FIGURE 168

REFRACTORS

There are two systems of lenses for refractors. The first was invented in the 17th century by Johannes Kepler, a German astronomer. The other was invented by the Italian scientist Galileo Galilei, also in the 17th century. If you trace the paths of light rays in Kepler's telescope (Fig. 168), you will see that they cross and therefore turn the image upside down and backward. This is not a serious problem if you use the telescope only in astronomy, because it makes no difference if you see a star upside down or right-side-up. It does make a difference in terrestrial telescopes, those used to look at things on earth. The image of an upside-down ship sailing in the wrong direction on an upside-down ocean is a problem. The eyepiece of Galileo's telescope was a double-concave lens (Fig. 169). It turned the image right-side-up and correctly from side to side. The same thing can be done by using two single-convex lenses.

Focusing a refracting telescope is done in the same way as focusing a microscope: the objective and eyepiece are moved farther apart or closer together until the image becomes clear.

All lenses have some problems of reproducing the color of objects accurately over the whole width of a lens. Also, lenses have the problem of twisting images out of shape near the edges of a lens. These problems can be solved for small lenses, but as the size of lenses is increased, so are the problems. Eventually, lenses reach a size at which they have serious problems that cannot be solved. So, there is a limit to the size of the objective lens that can be used in a refracting telescope.

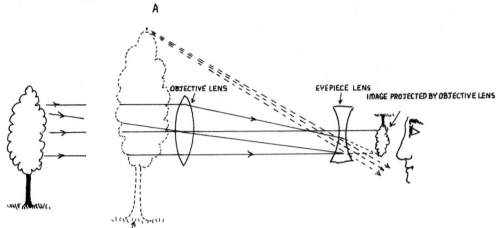

GALILEAN

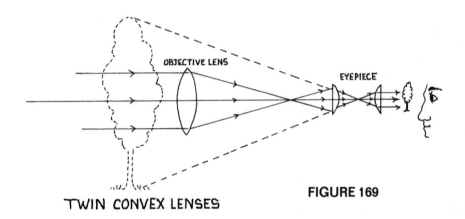

TWIN CONVEX LENSES

FIGURE 169

REFLECTORS

We can get around most of the lens problems of refractors with reflecting telescopes. In a reflector, a curved mirror takes the place of the objective lens of a refractor. Light entering the telescope strikes this mirror. The mirror forms a real image at a point where it can be magnified by the eyepiece.

The first reflecting telescope was built by the English scientist and mathematician, Isaac Newton. His type of reflector (Fig. 170) has a flat mirror that is almost, but not exactly, at the focus of the curved mirror. The flat mirror is set at an angle which causes it to reflect the image through a hole in the side of the tube. The eyepiece is fitted into this hole. You might suppose that the flat mirror would eliminate some of the light going to the eyepiece. Actually, it does, but not enough to make much difference.

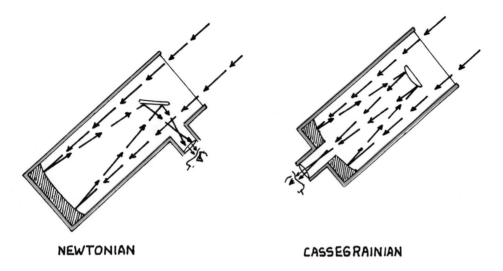

NEWTONIAN   CASSEGRAINIAN

FIGURE 170

Another kind of reflecting telescope was invented by the French physicist, N. Cassegrain, a few years after Newton made his reflector. In this telescope a large concave mirror at the rear of the tube gathers and reflects incoming light to a small convex mirror near the front. The convex mirror, in turn, reflects and focuses the light just a little behind a hole in a concave mirror where the eyepiece is located.

Most of the observations made through modern astronomical telescopes are done by photography. One reason for this is that photographic film can reveal details that the human eye can not see. A telescope is aimed at an object in the sky and is kept aimed there for hours by means of clockwork, turning the telescope to compensate for the rotation of the earth on its axis. During all of these hours, light too faint for the human eye to see builds up enough energy to form an image on photographic film. Also, special kinds of film can photograph stars and other objects in space that radiate infrared and ultraviolet light, neither of which the human eye can see. A device to hold photographic film is positioned where the eye would be if an astronomer were looking through the telescope. The lenses of the telescope act like lenses of a camera; they focus light on the film.

Light arriving at a telescope from galaxies billions of light years from the earth is very faint. One reason is that the light rays have diverged greatly as they traveled through space. Also, space contains vast amounts of tiny dust particles that block some of the light. To view or photograph faint stars and galaxies, we need a telescope with a lens arrangement that can pick up the faint light rays and concentrate them enough to provide

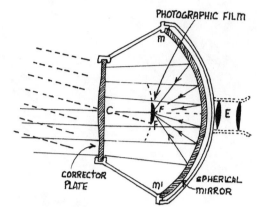

PHOTOGRAPHIC FILM

CORRECTOR PLATE

SPHERICAL MIRROR

FIGURE 171

KELLNER-SCHMIDT ASTRONOMICAL CAMERA

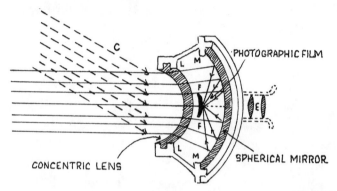

PHOTOGRAPHIC FILM

CONCENTRIC LENS

SPHERICAL MIRROR

FIGURE 172

MAKTUSOV ASTRONOMICAL CAMERA

the amounts of light needed for viewing or forming a photographic image. The Kellner-Schmidt (Fig. 171) and the Maktusov reflectors (Fig. 172) can do this best.

The purpose of the *corrector lens* in the Kellner-Schmidt system is to refract incoming parallel light rays so that after reflection from the curved mirror, M-M', they focus between points F and F'. Even if the rays enter the telescope slanted at a large angle (see broken lines), they still are brought to focus at F-F'. If you want to use the Kellner-Schmidt system for photography, you insert either a small piece of film at F-F' or a large piece between M and M'. If you want to use this telescope to observe the skies directly, you put a small curved mirror between F and F', have a hole in the center of the mirror M-M', and place an eyepiece, E, in the hole.

The Maktusov telescope does not need a corrector lens. It is an improvement on the Kellner-Schmidt reflector, because a corrector lens is difficult and expensive to make. The lens L-L' is simply part of a sphere, very accurately ground. The curve of the lens and of the mirror both have the same center, C. Therefore, they have the same curvature.

BINOCULARS

Binoculars are twin telescopes for use with both eyes at once. The telescopes are hinged to a post halfway between them, making it possible to widen or narrow the distance between them to fit the distance between the eyes.

There are two kinds of binoculars: *nonprismatic* and *prismatic*. Nonprismatic binoculars use only lenses. The prismatic kind use prisms (and possibly a mirror) along with the lenses.

NONPRISMATIC BINOCULARS

Among nonprismatic binoculars are *field glasses* and *opera glasses* (Fig. 173). Most of these have the arrangement of lenses invented by Galileo— a convex objective lens and a double-concave eyepiece lens. Instead of

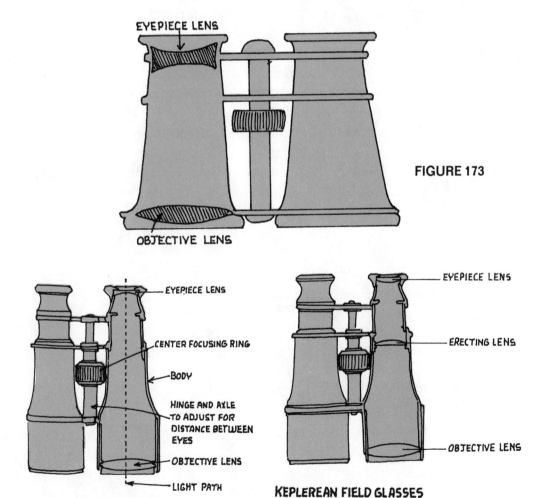

EYEPIECE LENS

FIGURE 173

OBJECTIVE LENS

EYEPIECE LENS

CENTER FOCUSING RING

BODY

HINGE AND AXLE TO ADJUST FOR DISTANCE BETWEEN EYES

OBJECTIVE LENS

LIGHT PATH

GALILEAN FIELD GLASSES

EYEPIECE LENS

ERECTING LENS

OBJECTIVE LENS

KEPLEREAN FIELD GLASSES WITH ERECTING LENS

the double-concave lens to turn the image upright and correctly from side to side, large nonprismatic field glasses have two sets of convex lenses between the objective and eyepiece lenses.

Opera glasses are the smallest and shortest binoculars. They have the smallest field of view, which means that the area you can see is not very wide. This is not a disadvantage, since opera glasses are used in a theater to magnify only a part of the stage at a time.

PRISMATIC BINOCULARS

Each telescope of prismatic binoculars is made up of two tubes. The tube holding the objective lens is to the side of, and in front of, the other (Fig. 174). Light entering the object lens is bent by prisms through two right angles before it enters the eyepiece lens. This arrangement has two advantages. First, it causes the light to travel much farther than it would if the telescopes were straight. Although the straight-line distance between the objective and eyepiece may be only 8 inches, the light travels almost 20 inches through the prisms, and makes possible a higher magnifying power for the same length of tube. Second, it sets the objective lenses farther apart, and makes the field of view much wider.

You may have seen binoculars described as 8 x 50, 10 x 60, or some similar combination of numbers. The first number represents the power of the telescopes, and the second the width of the objective lenses measured in millimeters. Descriptions of binoculars may also disclose the width of the field of view in feet when the telescopes are focused on an object 1,000 yards away.

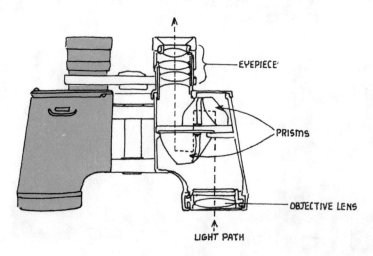

FIGURE 174

There are two ways to focus binoculars (Fig. 175). In one, a focusing ring on the post between the two telescopes is turned. The post consists of a hollow metal tube with a screw thread cut into its inner wall. A metal rod with a thread cut into it screws into the tube. The focusing ring is attached to the rod to make it easy to turn. The tubes that hold the eyepiece lenses of each telescope also are attached to the rod, and the tubes that hold the objective lenses are attached to the threaded tube. By turning the focusing ring, the eyepiece tubes move forward or backward in the objective tube until what you are looking at is in focus. This method is *center focusing*.

In the second way of focusing, each eyepiece lens is held in a short tube that has screw threads on its inside walls. These tubes screw onto the ones that hold the objective lenses. Turning each eyepiece tube moves it forward or backward. With this arrangement, you can focus each telescope separately to fit any difference in the vision of your eyes. This method is *individual focusing*.

CENTER FOCUS

FOCUSING RING

INDIVIDUAL FOCUS

INDIVIDUALLY FOCUSING EYEPIECES

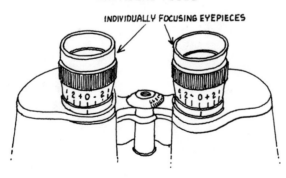

FIGURE 175

ZOOM LENSES

You have seen television or movie scenes in which the camera was focused on a far object—perhaps a house—and the camera seemed to move in until it was so close that you could see the face of a person in a window. In the early days of television, the cameraman and his camera actually rode on a wheeled platform that did move toward the house. Nowadays, when a camera seems to approach an object, the cameraman usually does not move. He uses a *zoom lens*, a kind of telescope that is mounted on the front of the camera. The magnifying power of this telescope can be increased or decreased by turning a crank that moves two pairs of lenses [shaded figures] within the tube (Fig. 176). These movements change the focal length continuously so that while the magnifying power of the lenses varies, the object is kept in focus. This is what your eyes do when you walk toward something you are looking at. However, the zoom lens does the same things without moving toward or away from the object being photographed.

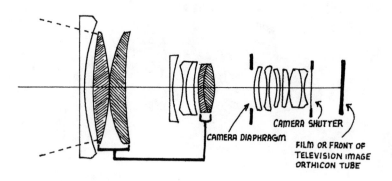

CAMERA DIAPHRAGM

CAMERA SHUTTER

FILM OR FRONT OF TELEVISION IMAGE ORTHICON TUBE

FIGURE 176

GLOSSARY

This glossary contains technical terms used in the text but not defined. It also contains words defined in one part of the text and used in another part without definition.

AILERON: a hinged control section on the trailing (rear) edge of an airplane wing.

AIRFOIL: a body having a cross section like the cross section of an airplane wing, and providing a lift force.

ALLOY: a metal that is a solution of two or more metallic elements, for example, brass, which is a mixture of the elements copper and zinc.

ALPHAMERIC, or ALPHANUMERIC: using both letters and numbers.

ALTIMETER: a device for measuring distance above sea level or above ground level.

ARBOR: an axle to which a gear or pinion is attached. *See* gear, pinion.

ARMATURE: the movable part of an electromagnetic device.

ATMOSPHERE: the envelope of air that surrounds the earth.

BAROMETER: a device for measuring the pressure of the atmosphere by means of the height of a column of mercury or the movement of a pointer on a dial.

BINARY SYSTEM: a number system having only two digits, 0 and 1.

BIT: contraction of the words *binary digit;* the unit of data stored in a computer, and depending on a choice between two alternative states, such as "on" or "off."

CHARACTER: one digit or letter.

CELSIUS, OR CENTIGRADE: a temperature scale in which 0° is at the freezing point of water and 100° at the boiling point of water at sea level; abbreviated C.

CIRCUIT: a combination of wires and other devices that conduct electric current from a source and back to the source.

CLUTCH: a coupling device used to connect the driving and the driven parts of a shaft.

COLLATOR: an automatic data processing machine that sorts punched cards, comparing them, changing their sequence, selecting or matching them.

CRANKSHAFT: a metal shaft made up of one or more cranks that directly transfers energy from a source such as an engine.

DATA: in data processing, facts used as a basis for processing.

DIGIT: one of the Arabic numerals from 0 to 9; also, one of the elements of a number system.

DIODE: a one-way electronic switch.

DOWNDRAFT: an area of falling air.

DRAG: the force produced by the resistance of air upon a body, such as an airplane, moving through it.

ELECTRIC CURRENT: the movement of electrons in a given direction in any material.

ELECTROMAGNET: an iron core surrounded by a coil of insulated wire through which an electric current is passed to produce a temporary magnet as long as the current flows.

ELECTRON: part of an atom; a unit of negative electricity.

ESCAPEMENT: the arrangement of gear wheel, fork-and-pallet, and balance wheel that causes a watch or clock to release energy from the mainspring in short, measured bursts.

EYEPIECE: the lens or system of lenses in an optical instrument that magnifies the image made by the objective lens. *See* objective. The lens nearest the eye.

FAHRENHEIT: a temperature scale in which the freezing point of water is at 32° and the boiling point is at 212° at sea level; abbreviated F.

FUSELAGE: the body of an airplane, minus wings and tail.

GENERATOR: a machine that changes mechanical energy into electrical energy in the form of electric current.

GEAR, OR GEAR WHEEL: a toothed wheel used to transmit motion from one turning shaft to another.

INFORMATION: in data processing, the result of processed data.

INPUT: data put into a data processing machine; also, the computer unit that changes data into a form that can be processed by the computer.

KEYPUNCH MACHINE: a data processing machine that punches holes in cards, either in response to keys struck by an operator, or automatically, as guided by a punched card.

LENS: a specially shaped piece of transparent material (usually glass) which is used to refract (bend) light rays in an optical instrument.

LIFT: the force that acts vertically upward on an aircraft, countering gravity.

LIFT PUMP: a pump that lifts liquid from a lower to a higher level, using atmospheric pressure.

LIGHT RAY: a bundle of light waves of no specific size or number.

LOGIC: in a computer, the interconnection of on/off circuits to represent the relationships of reasoned thinking.

MAGNETIC IRON OXIDE: a compound of iron and oxygen, found in nature, as an ore, that is very easily magnetized.

MAGNETIC INK: ink that contains magnetic iron oxide particles.

OBJECTIVE, or OBJECTIVE LENS: a lens that forms a real image in an optical instrument; the objective lens is the front lens.

OCULAR, or OCULAR LENS: another name for the eyepiece lens.

PHOTOCELL, or PHOTOELECTRIC CELL: a device that produces electric current when light shines on it; an "electric eye."

PITCH: (1) the distance advanced by a propeller in one revolution; (2) the angle with the horizontal made by helicopter blades; (3) the turning of an aircraft around a horizontal axis halfway between the nose and tail.

POWER: the rate of doing work, or the rate at which energy is transferred in doing work.

PRISM: transparent body with at least two flat surfaces that incline toward each other, and used to refract and reflect light.

PROCESSING: anything that is done with data in order to obtain information.

PROGRAM CARD: a punched card put into a keypunch machine to guide the machine in automatically punching other cards.

RATCHET WHEEL: a toothed wheel that can turn in one direction, but is prevented from turning in the opposite direction by a device that jams between two of the teeth.

READ: in data processing, to change the punches in cards, magnetized areas on tape, optical characters, or magnetized cores into electrical impulses that cause some part of a machine to move or move electrical impulses to be generated.

REFRACTION: the bending of light rays when passing from a less dense medium (such as air) into a more dense medium (such as glass), or when passing from a more dense to a less dense medium.

REGISTER: a temporary storage device for one machine (computer language) word in a computer.

RELATIVE WIND: the movement of air past an aircraft in flight.

ROLL: the turning of an aircraft about an axis that runs through the center of the fuselage from nose to tail. *See* pitch, yaw.

SENSOR: a device that responds to changes in conditions, such as temperature, light, or motion, and sends a signal to the controls of a machine or other device.

THROTTLE: the device that regulates the amount of fuel that goes to an aircraft engine.

THRUST: the force that moves an aircraft forward and which is produced by the engine.

TRANSPARENT: allowing light to pass through so that objects can be seen on the far side.

UPDRAFT: rapidly rising air.

YAW: the turning of an aircraft about a vertical axis between the nose and tail. *See* pitch, roll.

INDEX

216